TOWARD FREEDOM AND DIGNITY

O. B. HARDISON, jr.

TOWARD
FREEDOM
& DIGNITY

THE HUMANITIES
AND THE IDEA
OF HUMANITY

The JOHNS HOPKINS UNIVERSITY PRESS
Baltimore & London

The Johns Hopkins University Press, Baltimore, Maryland 21218
The Johns Hopkins University Press Ltd., London

Library of Congress Catalog Card Number 72-4010
ISBN 0-8018-1415-4 (clothbound edition)
ISBN 0-8018-1416-2 (paperbound edition)

Library of Congress Cataloging in Publication data
will be found on the last printed page of this book.

For Osborne and Matthew

If man is ever to solve that problem of politics in practice, he will have to approach it through the problem of the aesthetic, because it is only through Beauty that man makes his way to Freedom.

Friedrich Schiller, *Letters on
the Aesthetic Education of Man*

So it was, though I could not know it until I was done, that a theme developed. It grew almost directly out of the original choice and predilections. . . . The proper theme of the work, then, is the human imagination, the possibility, limits and variety of imaginative experience.

George Garrett, on writing
The Death of the Fox

CONTENTS

INTRODUCTION

y own generation grew up during the Great Depression and matured during Stalingrad, Cassino, Normandy, Hiroshima, the German death camps, and the betrayal of the Warsaw Ghetto. We have lived since then with the Cold War, the Hydrogen Bomb, the Population Explosion, Viet Nam, urban riots, and a decaying environment. Along with our burdens, however, we inherited one priceless treasure. In defiance of common sense and the plain evidence of history we were taught to regard crisis as exceptional. When we were still in kindergarten we learned from Herbert Hoover that prosperity is just around the corner. Just as doubts began to set in, Hoover's replacement assured us that the only thing we had to fear was fear itself.

Once learned, the habit of hope dies hard. Most of us, I suppose, cling to a kind of bitter optimism in spite of everything and would disagree with Cyril Connolly's gloomy prediction that in the future a man will be judged by the quality of his despair. But for large numbers of informed and intelligent people the optimism is wearing thin. I am not thinking only or even primarily of the socially dispossessed. I am thinking of the socially favored, of those who have sampled the best that modern society has to offer and found it lacking.

The uncertainty that is spreading through modern society is not a class phenomenon. It applies equally to conditions of life under socialism and capitalism. It is born from the difficult circumstances that surround our lives and from the enormous tensions—tensions between right and left, black and white, wealth and poverty, youth and age, and power and morality—created by these circumstances. These tensions assault us daily in newspaper headlines. They are manifested as well in countless small, hopeless acts of surrender that touch us personally—in copping out, in broken marriages, in drug addiction, in the forlorn communes that dot the American landscape, in acts of violence that are a baffling mixture of idealism and brutality, and in a listless, directionless apathy that craves any experience—from heroin to casual murder—as long as it holds the promise of being genuine experience.

The consciousness of the generation now reaching maturity was formed in the shadow of the apocalypse. Few of the traditions that our children inherited any longer fit the reality of their lives. Success appears to require obeisance to the very forces that sold them out. Patriotism, if it means concern for the well-being and honor of the nation, often seems to demand opposition to what the rule books call duly constituted authority. Personal relations are also changing. Marriage and the life-roles of women have been wrenched suddenly into new shapes by birth control and further modified by the pervasive, subliminal fear that to have children is to raise hostages to a savage future. Tradition itself, the accumulated wisdom of parents, teachers, and political leaders, has been undermined by the suspicion that there is little in previous human experience to guide us through the next half-century. As tradition is shattered by contact with reality, individuals find themselves baffled and isolated. The faces are still there gazing back from the mirrors of the self, but they are no longer reassuring. They are distorted, mocking, alien.

An adolescent who turns eighteen in 1972 will be forty-six in the year 2000. Yet the year 2000 seems more remote, more legendary than Homer's tale of the Fall of Troy 1200 years before Christ. Because the lives of those who will be forty-six in the year 2000 are only beginning, they are aware of its hazards in their bones. They are aware, as an older generation can never be, that the future may be winding down, that if there is a future it will be profoundly different from the present. Whether it is the Malthusian cataclysm forecast by writers like Paul Ehrlich and Jay W. Forrester or the geodesic Utopia of technocratic optimists like Buckminster Fuller, its physical conditions will be different and its mode of consciousness will be different.

The epigraph for the first postwar generation was anything but optimistic. It was written by T. S. Eliot in

The Hollow Men:

> This is the way the world ends,
> This is the way the world ends,
> This is the way the world ends,
> Not with a bang but a whimper.

Some thirty-five years later, when Allen Ginsberg spoke for the second postwar generation in *Howl*, the message was the same but the medium had heated up:

> I saw the best minds of my generation destroyed by madness, starving, hysterical, naked,
> dragging themselves through the angry streets looking for an angry fix,
> angelheaded hipsters burning for the ancient heavenly connection to the starry dynamo in the machinery of night.
> Who poverty and tatters and hollow-eyed and high sat up smoking in the supernatural darkness of cold water flats floating across the tops of cities contemplating jazz.

Evidently, for many people the apocalypse is already on our doorstep. It is here in enormous, inert bureaucracies consuming their energies in self-perpetuation. It is here in impersonal forces so powerful that they seem beyond human control. It is here in the subordination of men to things and abstractions. And it is here in the philosophy by which the subordination of men to things and abstractions is rationalized: a positivism whose first premise is that human beings are themselves things, that the human spirit is a ghost in a machine, a relic of the age of superstition, that the remedy for social problems—assuming there is a remedy—is to treat human beings like so many Pavlovian dogs, to be conditioned and programed into docile acceptance of a do-it-yourself blueprint of the Good Life.

It is probably quixotic to oppose an idea as fragile and as tentative as the idea of humanity to the enormous power of things and abstractions, but this is what I intend to do. The idea of humanity that I have in mind may gain stature, if not deterrent credibility, from the fact that it is a specific idea. It begins with the premise that the understanding of human concerns must be rooted not in things and abstractions but in the living, impermanent, and imperfect tissue of human experience. If so, the idea of humanity is intimately bound up with the questions and problems of aesthetics. Greek *aisthesthai* means "to perceive." To ask how inner and outer worlds are patterned on the delicate loom of the mind and given a unique tonality by the experiences and inadequacies of each individual mind is to ask the first question that any meaningful theory of human experience must pose for itself.

I mean this quite literally, and I mean it not only in relation to the individual but in relation to society as well. Hence the quotation from Schiller that stands at the beginning of this book: "If man is ever to solve that problem of politics in practice, he will have to approach it through the problem of the aesthetic, because it is only through Beauty that man makes his way to Freedom."

I wish to explore the idea and in a sense the methodology of freedom in modern, technological society. I could cite numerous antecedents in Plato and his followers and in Christian and non-Christian theology, but the concepts on which my analysis rests first emerged in a coherent, fully articulated position in the analysis of the relation of the mind to nature and the mediating function of human imagination worked out by Immanuel Kant at the end of the eighteenth century. Kant demonstrated that mind and nature are reciprocal. We cannot speak of an "interior world" that is subjective and an "exterior" that is objective. In fact, the idea of nature itself is meaningless except in relation to the imagination through which nature, with its myriad spiritual qualities of beauty, symmetry, color, relation, and symbolism, is created. The analysis of both the self and the surrounding world must start from an analysis of how both are perceived. The object of this analysis must be to determine the conditions under which the perception of the self and the world are harmonious—under which the self can expand creatively into the world, and the surrounding world appears to encourage rather than threaten this expansion.

This position is a form of humanism and it underlies a current of humanistic thought in education, history, aesthetics, and philosophy that has been continuous from Kant's lifetime to the present day. As Ernst Cassirer wrote in *The Logic of the Humanities*:

In the second half of the eighteenth century, in the period of classical German literature, a new humanism frees itself and begins to stand on its own feet; it has a totally different stamp and a far greater breadth and depth than Renaissance humanism. . . . For Winckelmann and Herder, for Goethe and Humboldt, and indeed, even for Schiller and Kant . . . the concept of humanity does not lie completely within the limits of the moral order. It extends to every creative act whatever, regardless of the particular sphere of life within which it realizes itself. Here there emerges *the fundamental feature of all human existence*, the fact that man is not lost within the welter of his internal impressions, that he learns to control this sea of impressions by giving it *ordered form*, which, as such, stems in the final analysis from himself, from his own thinking, feeling, and willing.

Since the dominant thrust of nineteenth- and twentieth-century society has been almost precisely opposite to this point of view, it has, for the most part, been critical. That is, it has opposed the values of modern society on the grounds that their abject surrender to things and abstractions denies man his freedom, strips him of his dignity, and leaves him an alien in his own world. The failure of modern society—its dehumanization of the working classes, its overreliance on technology, its corresponding indifference to traditional human values, and its use of overt and covert force as substitutes for the organic social forms once sustained by these values—are the evidence on which the humanistic critique of modern society rests.

Broadly defined, the humanities include both the

creative and the critical arts. In the wake of the Romantic movement the humanities have assumed the burden of objectifying the relation between the self and the world. This is most obvious in creative arts like poetry, painting, and music where the artist expresses his experience directly, but it is also true of critical arts like history, philosophy, and literary criticism, which involve contemplation of the transcript of human experience. In doing so, the humanities have, almost by definition, accepted responsibility for expressing the alienation between the self and the world that has characterized industrial and technological society. If artists from Blake to Picasso have given direct expression to this sense of alienation, it has been expressed no less powerfully by critics, philosophers, and historians from Coleridge to André Malraux. Although humanists are being joined increasingly by scientists appalled by the destructiveness of technological society, they remain today the most outspoken critics of modern culture, whether in the United States or the Soviet Union. And the humanities remain our most expressive means of objectifying the clash between the individual and the world which surrounds him.

Beyond their immediate concerns, what we learn from the humanities is that the human spirit is the fundamental fact of experience. The world that we regard as solid, determined, and material is a creation of the human spirit. Held up to the light of analysis, the world we experience is traced and veined with human value like a leaf held up to the sun. What we see is always and inevitably an aspect of ourselves. The world and the self are indeterminate. They are not what they are but what we individually and collectively make of them. Freedom is a condition of life. If we are dominated by things and abstractions this is not because we lack freedom but because we have cooperated in our own subjugation. To ignore this is the philosophical equivalent of performing brain surgery with a monkey wrench. You *can* perform brain surgery with a monkey wrench but the patient usually dies.

In a classic paper the physicist Werner Heisenberg showed that in certain situations the observer is involved in the supposedly objective events he is observing. Heisenberg called this the indeterminacy principle. It means that even in the pure sciences knowledge is always relative. What the observer discovers is a function of what he wants to discover.

The indeterminacy principle is significant as a philosophical principle in the pure sciences, but it is a central fact of life in the social and psychological sciences. It is involved in all efforts to quantify and measure human experience. This is true in biology, psychology, and the social sciences, and its validity has been demonstrated time and again in the humanities through a long series of self-defeating efforts to place humanistic studies on an objective basis. The questions of an interviewer always influence the answers he receives. The assumptions underlying a survey always shape the data gathered. The personality of the psychoanalyst necessarily affects the response of the patient. And an analysis of the imagery of *Paradise Lost* ultimately depends on the critic's definition of an image, even though he writes in Fortran IV and stores his information in a computer. Predictions are self-fulfilling, and where everything can be measured, to decide what is worth measuring is to determine the image of reality that emerges after the measurements have been taken.

It is not that we are free to choose but that we are not free to avoid choice. In spite of the trappings of objectivity in which we like to drape our psychological, educational, social, and artistic theories, the knowledge they have to offer is always indeterminate in the sense of being relative to the values behind them. When we ask for objective solutions to social or artistic problems, we are asking for brain surgery with a monkey wrench. Of course we have asked for objective solutions and the results have often been sorry witness to the perversity of the demand. We have used (and are using) genetic theories to justify racism, psychology to undermine one social class and reinforce another, economics to restructure traditional social relations in terms of arbitrary concepts of what constitutes the Good Life, and all the sciences for ways to avoid responding directly, in human terms, to the values of art. In such cases our idea of humanity, our sense of what it is to be human and what human beings need to live with dignity and purpose, has been sacrificed to abstractions. The eighteenth-century philosophers blamed this habit on religion. In the twentieth century we have exchanged the dogmatism of religion for the universal dogmatism of political ideology and the lesser dogmas of the social planners and the psychologists.

What we desperately need today is an alternative, a counterweight to dogmas and abstractions, an idea of humanity against which we can measure our grand designs for progress. Only by constantly renewing our sense of what it is to be radically and simply human, will we retain the vision—and the humility—necessary to avoid becoming victims of our theories of what we ought to be. We crave survival with all the intensity of instinct. Faced with prison or oblivion, most of us would choose the first. But survival is a poor value without the freedom and dignity and beauty that give life its meaning. A society without these values will be a concentration camp for sullen, rebellious inmates, or a psychiatric ward for patients made docile by spiritual lobotomy. This is what Schiller meant when he wrote that the problem of politics can be solved only through the problem of aesthetics. The occasion for his observation was his disillusionment with the French Revolution. His words are as valid now as when Robespierre and the Jacobins first discovered that the road to liberty, equality, and fraternity led up the steps of the guillotine, with the difference that the failure of the French Revolution was a European phenomenon, while the failure of modern culture is a global failure.

In spite of everything, the humanities remain obstinately, radically human. They teach us what it is to be human, and they teach us directly, through immediate experience. What we gain from them is not an accumulation of facts but an enlargement of our own humanity. They do not guarantee the survival of the species, but they do provide conditions necessary to the life of the spirit. They do not swell the Gross National Product, but they enrich the lives of individuals and deepen the sense of community among men and cultures. They are more obviously related to the past than the future, but they create the perspective—perhaps the only perspective—within which a viable human future can be imagined.

If this point of view is worth considering, and if the bitter optimism that is the habit of my generation is anything more than wishful thinking, the future of the humanities is a subject of the broadest general interest. It certainly involves the humanities as they are institutionalized in the educational system. But it also involves modern culture itself—where it is, where it seems to be moving, and what it might be if we manage to avoid World War III on the one hand and *1984* on the other.

The view of the humanities taken here is derived ultimately from Romantic philosophy, especially Kant's *Critique of Judgment* (1790) and Schiller's great but neglected *Letters on the Aesthetic Education of Man* (1795). As will be evident, I feel the tradition is still strong, whatever its mutations, in such contemporary works as Ernst Cassirer's *The Logic of the Humanities*, the closely reasoned work of a professional philosopher, and A. S. Neill's *Summerhill*, the impassioned and empirical testimony of a modern educator.

The chapters of this book form a triptych. I wanted to begin with problems that were quite specific and therefore easy to illustrate. The first two chapters therefore deal with the plight of the humanities in the academy. The academy is neither a sanctuary nor an ivory tower; it is a microcosm of the culture around it. That the humanities have traditionally occupied an important place in the academy reflects the fact that they have traditionally been considered important (for both right and wrong reasons) by society. The fact that they are in trouble reflects a growing dehumanization of that society.

The third and fourth chapters are historical. They deal with root confusions about the role of the humanities in culture that have persisted from the Renaissance to the present. Inevitably, they are confusions that have had damaging effects on the lives of individuals, whether the individuals have been heroic figures like Petrarch or Milton or Schiller, torn between the claims of art and ideology, or twentieth-century schoolchildren trapped in a system based on theories about what human beings ought to be rather than what they are.

The last two chapters look beyond the present. The fifth attempts to outline the shape of a possible future society, drawing on an abundant literature dealing with social changes that are likely in the coming decades. The sixth returns to direct experience. It is the personal record of an attempt to develop humanistic values in a single literature class devoted to a single author. My strategy was very modest and involved no root-and-branch changes in the institution where I was teaching when I worked it out, but it convinced me that education properly understood can be a significant influence—an active force rather than a passive microcosm— in shaping the surrounding culture.

My major contention is simple. The humanities are vitally important to our society. I have stated what seem to me to be the essential values of the humanities. They are the spiritual values of freedom, dignity, and beauty, and the critical values of openness, toleration, and a measured skepticism of all dogmas. I have not attempted anything that could be described as a program. There are programs in abundance for both humanizing and dehumanizing modern society, and I assume my readers will be familiar with many of them. I wanted instead to concentrate on a few issues and to place them in a historical context sufficient to bring them into focus. Here, if anywhere, is my claim to bringing something new to subjects that have already been discussed often and with great intelligence. I will add that while I obviously disagree with many contemporary authorities, I have tried to make my case directly, with a minimum of rebuttal of opposing points of view. When I have cited opinions with which I differ, I have generally done so for illustration rather than formal refutation. Although most of what is included here was written before B. F. Skinner's *Beyond Freedom and Dignity* was published, my title was chosen after the fact. It seemed to me important to underscore the divergence between the tradition for which Dr. Skinner is such an able and persuasive spokesman and the fundamentally different tradition underlying my own thought on cultural matters. When we are so far from achieving a society in which there is an adequate measure of freedom and dignity, it seems to me at the very least premature to discuss moving beyond them.

This book was originally delivered as a series of lectures at the annual Humanities Forum sponsored by Elon College in North Carolina. The remarkable dedication of the Elon students and their faculty adviser Dr. James Elder to the work of the forum is itself persuasive evidence of the continuing importance of the humanities in this country. I am personally grateful to the college and to Dr. Elder, for without the invitation to speak, generously renewed for three consecutive years, I would not have had the opportunity to bring together the ideas presented in the following pages.

In keeping with the lecture format, I have tried to be plain rather than technical and to give important citations in the text rather than in footnotes. If I have occasionally strayed from the normal territory of the scholar, teacher, and librarian, I have attempted to support my positions with the testimony of those who, presumably, know. I offer special thanks to Dr. Richmond Crinkley, Director of Programs at the Folger Library, for reading the text in manuscript and offering many useful suggestions, and to Miss Margaret Enzler, also of the Folger, for generous assistance in preparing the final copy for the printer.

CHAPTER 1

What has happened then is that the new generation's rejection of authority, of scholarship, knowledge, and culture has shaken their professors' confidence in their own intellectual and moral authority. If in some academicians, confidence in their intellectual and moral authority borders on arrogance and cultural imperialism, in others loss of confidence has led, in effect, to abdication of responsibility.

Morris B. Abram, speech at Davidson College,
October, 1971

But the teacher, as Plato's dialogues illustrate so beautifully, must do more than simply start where his students are; he must also take them somewhere else. To do that, he must have some convictions about where they should go, convictions, that is to say, about what is worth learning.

Charles Silberman, *Crisis in the Classroom*

NO POSSUM, NO SOP, NO TATERS;
OR, A LACK OF CASH AND
A FAILURE OF NERVE

I have borrowed the title of a poem by Wallace Stevens for this chapter because it expresses, with saving irony, the current situation of the humanities in America. It is not a unique situation. Throughout our history, our attitudes toward the humanities have been ambivalent. We have ridiculed the humanities as useless, trivial, affected—even un-American—distractions from the real business of life. At the same time, we have accepted them as the basis of general education and as the core subjects around which the undergraduate curriculum should be organized.

Often the hostility and the respect have been curiously mingled. American innocents have never tired of making fun of the culture they found abroad, but neither have they ceased going abroad. And the same businessmen who have announced from the board room and the golf course that culture is a waste of time have, for the past century, been sending their sons to Harvard, Yale, and Princeton at great expense to learn French and German and read the classics from Plato to Kafka.

Today, however, the situation of the humanities is especially precarious. There are several reasons for this. Since the nineteenth century the standing of the humanities in relation to other disciplines has been declining. As new disciplines have emerged and older ones like physics and economics have expanded, the humanities have been pushed from the center to the side and even to the periphery of the curriculum.

More recently, the disruptions that began on the campus and in the city in 1965 had the effect of concentrating national attention on social issues. While the humanities continued to languish, showers of saint-seducing gold were rained on programs of social action. Concern for social problems also had its effect within the humanities. Traditional programs were attacked as irrelevant to current needs, and new ones, intended to meet the challenge of relevance, were introduced. In spite of some healthy reforms, the net effect has been widespread confusion and a deepening sense of futility among professional humanists.

While the humanities were still trying to adjust to the creed of relevance, the recession that began in 1969 changed the ground rules of American education. Everyone has suffered from the recession, but the humanities have been particularly vulnerable. With the replacement of educational philosophy by cost accounting, small classes have been eliminated, average class size has grown, research funds have been cut, and whole departments have disappeared with no other epitaph than "They didn't pay their way."

Given this situation, what is the future of the humanities? Are they relics of a pretechnocratic age? Vestigial organs that will atrophy as society evolves toward newer and presumably higher forms? Are they impediments to progress that should be demolished root and branch? Or do they represent a heritage so important that to lose it would be to lose the very qualities that make men greater than the systems they devise and mark the difference between a society of robots and a community of civilized human beings?

These questions are large and abstract. But they have immediate practical consequences. Our answers affect national policy, the allocation of government and private funds, the shape of the curriculum from kindergarten to graduate school, and ultimately, the shape of our culture. Should we train students broadly or narrowly—for life, as the progressive educators have it, or for jobs? Should education be understood as the assimilation of information—in which case, mass lectures, standardized testing, performance contracts, and a "national video university" would be acceptable? Or should education be understood as the assimilation of values—in which case the new English primary schools described in the Plowden Report of 1967, with their emphasis on small groups and intrapersonal relationships, might be a model? To turn from social policy to people, since a student must choose among many courses and taking one course means not taking another, should he be advised to register for Shakespeare or Urban Sociology, a seminar in Plato or an introduction to computer programming? Will a future lawyer benefit more from studying north Italian painting of the Renaissance or Keynesian economic theory? A doctor from *Hamlet* or differential equations? These are real choices. Over a period of four years they add up to the kind of education a student receives and, by extension, to the values that he takes from the academy into society.

II   In 1964 the Commission on the Humanities, a group sponsored by the American Council of Learned Societies that included several of the most distinguished American humanists then active, issued the report that led to the establishment of the National Endowments for the Arts and Humanities. The report included the following statement:

During our early history we were largely occupied in mastering the physical environment. No sooner was the mastery within sight than advancing technology opened up a new range of possibilities, putting a new claim on energies which might otherwise have gone into humane and artistic endeavor. The result has often been that our social, moral, and aesthetic development lagged behind our material advance. . . . The state of the humanities today creates a crisis for national leadership. While it offers cultural opportunities of the greatest value to the United States and to mankind, it holds at the same time a danger that wavering purpose and lack of well-conceived effort may leave us second-best in a world correspondingly impoverished by our incomplete success.

Today these words have a quaintness that we normally associate with kerosene lamps and Smith Brothers Cough Drops. Evidently, the members of the Commission harbored no doubts about the basic soundness of the humanities. The chief problem was financial and the ingenious solution they hit upon was government money. More money would presumably do the same thing for the humanities that the National Science Foundation had done for the sciences after Sputnik. In the academy this would mean more courses, more teachers, more research, and of course, more influence. In society it would mean more artists, more dance companies and orchestras, more theater companies, and more libraries. Everybody would be edified. Our "social, moral, and aesthetic development" would catch up to our material progress, and we would no longer have to worry about being second-best or about our incomplete success contributing to international cultural deprivation.

The Commission was undoubtedly on the side of the angels and as American as cherry pie in proposing to solve its problems with government money, but it was wrong in assuming that the humanities were basically sound. Since 1965 they have been criticized and attacked from every conceivable angle. Apprehensions over their soundness are evident in the debate over teaching versus research and its cousin the publish-or-perish controversy; in the popularity of cost accounting, accountability, and performance contracts; in the appearance of "store-front schools," "free universities" and work-study programs based on the premise that the official curriculum is sterile and elitist; and in unprecedented—and unprecedentedly popular—experimentation with new courses, new degree requirements, new methods, and new subject categories cutting across previously impenetrable departmental barriers.

III   This turbulence is obviously not simply an educational problem. The academy has no control whatever over the growth of knowledge. Yet knowledge has grown geometrically since the beginning of the twentieth century. As the curriculum has expanded to keep up with this growth, the relative standing of the humanities has declined. In the period between 1901 and 1910, 28 percent of all Bachelor's degrees were in the humanities. In 1951–53 the figure had fallen to 15 percent. The corresponding decline in Doctoral degrees was from 33 to 16 percent. Thus, while absolute enrollment in the humanities has increased, the humanities have been steadily losing ground to other disciplines.

The loss per se is not especially worrisome. There is no reason why every college student should major in English or philosophy, just as there is no reason why a chemistry student should not appreciate (and even take courses in) literature or music or fine art. Along with the loss in status, however, has come an increasing tendency to question the idea of education posed by the humanities.

For the present I will refer to this idea as "general education." As recently as thirty years ago general education provided the rationale for the college preparatory track of the high schools and the first two years of undergraduate studies. Typically, it involved extensive work in English, foreign languages, and history, together with mathematics and a scattering of basic courses in the sciences. Only after an extended period of generalized study was the student allowed to proceed to a major. Often it was argued that students should not specialize at all, since education should prepare them for a variety of responsibilities rather than for a single vocation.

Memories of this tradition linger on. We read in the preamble of the catalogue of an exclusive New England college:

Whatever the form of experience . . . intellectual competence and awareness of problems are the goal of the program, rather than direct preparation for some profession.

Morris B. Abram, former President of Brandeis University, explains the ideal in a speech given at Davidson College:

Higher liberal education has, I believe, one primary and proper function: to teach those students who have the capacity and desire to learn from books *how* to learn. An education which accomplishes this in the student equipped for and desiring it is, I submit, always and thoroughly relevant. It provides the so-educated man or woman with the skills to make the learning relevant.

An example: At the outbreak of World War II, Oliver Franks, later Ambassador to the United States, was a tutor of moral philosophy at Queens College, Oxford. He was called from that

post to become Permanent Secretary of the Ministry of Supply—
the head of British war production industries.

What qualified him for the position was not any special training;
it was, rather, having the mind, character, and ability to learn—in
this case something as far afield from moral philosophy as the
management of British industry.

Although the memories linger, the design has faded.
The old courses and departments have been joined by a
host of new courses and departments in fields like political science, anthropology, economics, sociology, public
health, psychology, and city planning, to name the obvious ones. Many of these were not even listed in college
catalogues thirty years ago. Our cultural perspective has
also broadened. The original general education curriculum seldom strayed beyond the limits of Western culture. Today we think in terms of world culture rather
than national culture, and in terms of the relation of
disciplines rather than their separation. Meanwhile, the
system of allocating the first two years of college to
general studies and the last two to specialization, together with the network of requirements that prevented
early concentration, has dissolved. Junior colleges tend
to stress vocational training, and four-year colleges vacil-
late between the extreme of no requirements and the
opposite extreme of permitting major work to begin
during the freshman year.

Instead of producing a more coherent curriculum, the
demise of general education has left a vacuum. Shortly

before the semester begins at a typical American college
the student is presented with a catalogue listing hun-
dreds of different courses. If he is lucky he may be able
to arrange a fifteen-minute conference with a harried
faculty adviser. If not, he does the best he can on his
own. The humanities, in other words, no longer provide
a core around which higher education—or even a two-
year segment of it—is organized. Instead, they are one of
a number of special-interest groups competing for programs, courses, students, and money.

Recent national and international events are as far
beyond the control of the academy as the growth of
knowledge. Yet these events also generate pressures that
affect the curriculum. Most obviously, the pressure of
events resulted, after Sputnik and the urban riots, in
lavish financing of the sciences and social sciences.
Administrators who paid lip service to the value of the
humanities paid hard cash to attract faculty members
whose work fell "within the national interest," to quote
the magic phrase. This does not mean that the administrators were Philistines or hypocrites, merely that they
were not free agents. They necessarily based their decisions on committee recommendations and money. As
the number of humanists on their committees dwindled,
the priorities of the committees changed. As for money,
until very recently a faculty member whose work was in
the national interest was an investment. He could usually raise more than he was paid, and the money he
raised bought more facilities, more students, and more

faculty members who, in turn, sat on the committees that made curriculum recommendations. The circle was not vicious because it was not consciously antihumanistic, but it was undeniably circular.

In 1960, the President's Advisory Committee on Science warned:

> While the report centers on the needs of science, we repudiate emphatically any notion that science research and scientific education are the only kinds of learning that matter in America. . . . Even in the interests of science itself it is essential to give full value to the other great branches of man's artistic, literary, and scholarly activity. The advancement of science must not be accomplished by the impoverishment of anything else.

Alas, during the New Frontier and the Great Society there was little time to ponder this warning. Congress supported the Peace Corps, the Job Corps, the Teacher Corps, the Space Program, the Model Cities Program, Medicare, the War on Poverty, and a whole alphabet of crash programs under the Department of Health, Education and Welfare. Typically, when the humanities were involved in these federal initiatives the programs were action-oriented. There was scant sympathy for the "artistic, literary, and scholarly activities" mentioned by the President's Committee. Within the government, the only bright spots in an otherwise bleak picture are the National Endowments for the Arts and the Humanities. As for the private sector, the major foundations have had their moments of generosity, but the pattern of their grants has resembled that of the federal government, with emphasis on international relations, minority problems, and the difficulties of the inner city.*

The distortions introduced by lopsided funding have been exaggerated by human frailty. During the flush period of outside money, administrators often fell into the trap of competing for grants regardless of how they were to be used. Programs were created ad hoc or, alternately, they were sold to the academy by foundation hucksters dazzled by their personal theories of what was relevant or innovative or simply newsworthy. As the financial tide ebbed, many of these jury-rigged programs collapsed, and the colleges have been left to pick up the pieces. Since professors have tenure and hardware must be maintained even though nobody uses it, colleges have had to use operating funds to cover the cost of past venality. Institutional priorities have been warped to fit the realities of the budget. In contests between the Comptroller and the Dean of Humanities, it goes without saying who has usually won.

Confused by these excursions and alarums, students may be pardoned for failing to insist on the value of the humanities, and within the past few years there has been

---

*According to Mr. H. Ronald Rouse, Director of the Woodrow Wilson Foundation, government support for graduate study has fallen from 11,000 fellowships in 1968/69 to a projected 1,500 in 1972/73. This occurs at a time when the Woodrow Wilson Fellowship program, chiefly supported by Ford, has been terminated, and when the Fulbright program, for the humanities one of the most significant government programs ever authorized by the Congress, has been drastically curtailed.

a shift away from them in favor of the more obviously "relevant" curricula of the social sciences. The out-migration has been accelerated by the disappearance of the entrance and degree requirements that made general education work. Foreign languages have been the chief immediate victims, but in the long run all studies that depend on the use of more than one language—and this includes most advanced studies in the humanities—will suffer.* Foreign languages were once officially considered "in the national interest." In spite of former government and foundation support and a great deal of pious rhetoric, we have evidently now concluded that they are a personal rather than a social concern.

IV If we turn from the political and social context within which the humanities exist to the humanities themselves, it is clear that outer pressures are complemented by inner stresses. Some of these are as old as education itself. Others—the most disturbing—are new.

Here, a little perspective will be useful. Educational philosophy has historically moved in three quite distinct directions. I will call these liberal, vocational, and aesthetic. Since I will be discussing them again later in this book I will limit myself to a brief sketch of each.

*Foreign language enrollments fell from 17.6 percent of all college enrollments in 1965 to 12.6 percent in 1970 and have continued to decline since then, while between 1965 and 1970 about 45 percent of American colleges abolished or reduced their foreign language requirements according to a survey by Richard Brod in the September 1971 issue of the ADFL *Bulletin.*

Liberal education goes back to the Renaissance, which in turn derived it from Greek and Roman sources. It was originally a curriculum for grammar schools rather than universities (which were unknown before the Middle Ages), and the term "liberal" refers to the fact that this sort of education was considered appropriate for members of a particular social class, free citizens in contrast to slaves. Renaissance humanists made liberal education the basis of their curriculum because they wanted to create an intellectual elite. The Renaissance ideal of the *uòmo universale*—the man conversant with all aspects of his world—led them to stress general rather than specialized education, and the ideal of *mens sana in corpore sano*—a sound mind in a sound body—led them to insist that physical exercise, from wrestling and fencing to dancing, be a part of the curriculum. These ideas are still with us today—in the concept of *litterae humaniores*, the classics of literature, history, and philosophy that underlie the "great books" courses once common on American campuses, as well as in the physical education courses through which most of us suffered during freshman and sophomore years.

The most frequent explanation for liberal education, whether in the Renaissance or the twentieth century, is that it produces the ethical values and mental disciplines necessary for leadership. (Recall Oliver Franks's exemplary ascent from a professorship of moral philosophy to the Ministry of Supply.) At its best, liberal education is an effort to live up to Plato's ideal in *The Laws*: "If

you want to know what is the good in general of education the answer is easy: education produces good men
and good men act nobly." In practice, the concern with
ethics and leadership involves compromises. Liberal education typically thinks of leadership within the established order, and its modern strongholds have been
establishment universities—Oxbridge in England and the
Ivy League in America. It tends therefore to be conservative. Whatever its values, however, whether conservative or leftist, the more they are stressed the more liberal education tends to become a form of indoctrination. The subjects studied—in particular the liberal
arts—become less important than the ideology they are
used to convey.

Second, there is vocational education. Vocational
education is as old as the apprentice system. It was institutionalized in the wake of the industrial revolution.
According to the vocationists, liberal education is elitist.
It is a gentleman's game. It does nothing to train people
for jobs or to promote the greatest good for the greatest
number. The proper task of education is to create economically useful skills. It helps people earn their livings,
or to look at it from another angle, it provides recruits
for expanding industries. Those with limited talents
should be educated in trade schools, while the more
promising should attend universities to be trained as
engineers, chemists, physicans, architects, lawyers, and
business executives. The legacy of this philosophy is evident in the United States in vocational schools, in the

system of college majors oriented toward socially desirable skills, and in polytechnic universities, with MIT, Cal Tech, and VPI among the obvious examples.

Third, there is aesthetic education. I use the term for lack of a better one; in later chapters I will refer to it simply as humanistic education. The aesthetic point of view regards the experience of the individual as an absolute. It does not attempt to instill any particular ideology, nor is it interested in the economic utility of what is learned. Insofar as it has a curriculum it tends to emphasize the humanities. Its distinctive feature is not subject matter but its attitude toward subject matter. Beauty is its own excuse for being, and poetry makes nothing happen, but happens, itself, in a way that is important to the reader. From this point of view, the central value of education should be the freedom of the individual and the enlargement and enrichment of his inner life.

These three philosophies of education exist today in innumerable mixtures and variations. In general, the advocates of liberal education and the vocationists agree on a basic issue: the humanities exist to be used. If they neither teach an ideology nor create job skills they are not worth the effort. This is the opposite of the aesthetic position, which regards the humanities as self-justifying ends. You do not read *Macbeth* to learn about the evils of ambition and hence become a better committeeman or a less pushy second vice president. You read *Macbeth* because the experience is worthwhile. It is better in an absolute sense to have read *Macbeth* than not to have read it.

This brings us back to the pressure of events. If recent events have pressed in on the academy from the outside, they have also affected those within the academy. As demands for direct social action have become more urgent, there has been a loss of direction among humanists that is essentially a loss of confidence in the humanities as self-justifying ends. The burden of the complaint is that the humanities—or the humanities as taught—make no direct contribution to civil rights or ending the war in Viet Nam or the class struggle or Women's Liberation or whatever happens to be the cause of the moment.

In a widely publicized article in the March 1966 issue of *Harper's* magazine entitled "The Shame of the Graduate Schools," William Arrowsmith calls humanistic education "pathetically wanting—timid, unimaginative, debased, inefficient, futile." He adds that "the humanists have betrayed their subject" because they have permitted or encouraged a "gulf between one's studies and one's life, between what we read and how we live." If the times demand action, the argument runs, let the humanists become activist too. If they fail to do so they are escapist and irresponsible—"debased, inefficient, futile."

As the times have become more critical, the summons to action has become louder and the denunciations more vitriolic. For Louis Kampf, a former President of the Modern Language Association of America, Arrowsmith's "shame" has become an "open scandal." In "The Scandal of Literary Scholarship" published in *Harper's* of December 1967, Mr. Kampf announces the demise of his profession with grim satisfaction:

Of the death of academic literary study as a serious enterprise few seem to be aware. Yet in spite of appearances to the contrary, it is a fact. . . . As one looks at the body it wriggles and twitches. . . . A closer examination reveals an army of vermin in frantic development.

Like Arrowsmith, Kampf demands a payoff from humanistic study:

Today the idea of independent scholarship is a mask for the commercial activities of the academic bureaucracy. . . . If literary scholarship is to have an effect it must be committed to an end. . . . Commitment to what? Surely not to imprinting a static literary tradition on the minds of victims trapped in a classroom, nor to instilling in them a servile admiration for the glories of the past. Our devotion to criticism demands a willingness to destroy received dogmas, to rid ourselves of the deadening burden of history.

And again:

For my students to react fully to the *Dunciad* . . . it may be more important for them to consult Marx's work on the cultural effects of Capitalism than Aubrey Williams' useful study of the poem's

literary context; the former will channel their aesthetic percep-
tions into social understanding and (perhaps) action; the latter,
into literary analysis.

Kampf's disdain for literary analysis leads to another
point. The zeal aroused by the pressure of events has
turned many humanists against themselves and their
subjects. Fifty years ago, Irving Babbitt, in many ways
the finest literary critic of his generation, was led by his
political conservatism to condemn the major French
writers of the nineteenth century—among others, Victor
Hugo, Baudelaire, Verlaine, and Balzac. Kampf's equally
fervent Marxism leads him to reject the main tendencies
of twentieth-century literature:

The narcissistic obsession of modern literature for the self, the
critical cant concerning the tragic isolation of the individual—
these are notions which tie our hands and keep us from the
communion necessary for meaningful action.

If these remarks seem extreme, they are no more so
than a comment by Seymour Krim in *The New York
Times Book Review* of April 14, 1968, which typifies
both the attitude and the rhetoric of activism. Commenting on W. H. Auden's line "poetry makes nothing
happen," Krim writes:

Mr. Elliott and Headmaster Auden want to stick [literature]
under glass or in the freezer, in the over-civilized conceit that it is
too good for action out in the riot-torn cities. . . . Perhaps the

entire balance of our country and the new values we need to redeem ourselves as a once-decent people hinge on great and vengeful words that are also art.

The extent to which these attitudes have permeated the humanities is illustrated by statements made at a meeting of chairmen of English departments by John Fisher, Secretary from 1961 to 1971 of the largest organization of humanists in the United States. In 1969 Fisher told the chairmen that English departments are "inextricably bound in with an elitist principle" and that if this elitist principle is not accepted "the English department may be worse than useless. It may be the dead hand of the past inhibiting the development of the attitudes and ideas of a new society." He added, "The subject of English in this country has been used to inculcate a white, Anglo-Saxon, Protestant ethic. . . . My own feeling is that the game is just about played out." This is not the opinion of a political radical who accidentally blundered into teaching literature, but of a moderate and respected scholar who, at the time he expressed it, had been official spokesman for 30,000 humanists for eight years.

There is nothing new about the kind of anti-intellectualism that reduces all value judgments to questions of ideology. It is as old as Plato's decision to ban Homer from his ideal Republic because of Homer's impure religious and moral attitudes. It is unpleasant but harmless when expressed by a private individual. It is more disturbing when it is expressed by the chief officer of a major professional society, since it can hardly fail to demoralize half of his followers and turn the other half into instant Jeremiahs. When upheld by a powerful organization like the state, it becomes dangerous. It is the standard justification for censorship, the persecution of dissident artists, and the banality of official themes and styles. It has been invoked regularly to justify the imprisonment, exile, and execution of artists in totalitarian and Communist states; it has been invoked sporadically but often viciously in the United States, as, for example, in the persecution of leftist artists during the McCarthy period or the recent refusal by the American Academy of Arts and Sciences to award Ezra Pound a prize for literary achievement recommended by the Academy's own Committee on awards.

In spite of this fact, and in spite of the object lesson provided by the plight of Russian artists and the fatuity of official art, whether of the right or the left, the demand for relevance is widespread. Pursuits that do not promise immediate social benefits are unpopular. The effects of the external pressures on the humanities are thus magnified by the antihumanistic polemics of the humanists themselves.

V So much for the possum and the sop. When we come to the taters we encounter two additional problems—the multiplication of humanities courses and methodologies.

I will discuss the first problem in the next chapter. For now, I will merely observe that a curriculum with a limited number of courses, few electives, and interdisciplinary reinforcement—so that, for example, a basic history course is coordinated with a basic literature course—may not be ideal but it is at least coherent. As course offerings multiply, coordination becomes increasingly difficult. A student spends more and more time on less and less. His courses, even within his major, become isolated and unrelated. Eventually it becomes possible to ask whether the program itself is not a myth; or whether, granted its existence, it adds up to anything worthwhile.

As for methodology, over the years the humanities have accumulated an almost embarrassing number of methods, but no single method has turned up that will answer all or even most of the questions that humanists like to ask. Faced with the options of philology, historical criticism, comparative criticism, *Quellengeschichte*, stylistics, genre theory, structuralism, contextualism, myth criticism, Freudian analysis, the sociology of literature, and phenomenology, to name only a few possibilities, most humanists are inclined to sympathize with the advice given by Henry James to a young man who asked him how one writes good novels: "Be very intelligent." To James's intelligence I would add a second criterion—sensitivity—if the two are not really different sides of the same coin.

But intelligence and sensitivity are not enough for critics of the humanities who want a single foolproof method and an objective way of measuring the payoff. At times almost everyone has gotten into this act with results ranging from high comedy to tragedy. An attractive and, in some ways, a very conservative critique is offered by Professor W. O. Maxwell in an article in the March 1968 issue of the *Bulletin* of the American Association of University Professors entitled "The Methodological Plight of the Humanities." Professor Maxwell asks:

What is the nature of the link between the subject matter of the humanities and the goals they espouse? I suggest we don't know, and that from that fact stems, in large measure, the plight of the humanities. . . . Because of this methodological gap, research in the humanities lacks purpose and direction. . . . there are no set criteria with which to judge the method used in research or its results, so that much of this research is not cumulative.

And a little later:

The . . . gap between the humanities and the goals of the humanities limits the ways in which curricula . . . can develop. . . . We cannot objectively specify the subject matters, mastery of which furthers these goals more than other subject matters.

Apostles of accountability to the contrary, a sympathetic student of the humanities might regard Maxwell's comments as the beginning of wisdom. He has stated an important truth about the humanities and specified quite clearly what they cannot do. But Maxwell is an adversary, not an advocate. From his point of view the humanities should have specific goals, a method for reaching these goals, and a way of measuring whether they have or have not been attained. What he fails to see is that for humanistic study his criteria are a liability. Any attempt to establish objective goals—as against subjective and individual ones—leads the humanities back in the direction of Irving Babbitt and Louis Kampf—to the elitist values of the right or the Marxist *Dunciad*; that is, to orthodoxy as the test of artistic excellence and propaganda in place of teaching.

In a way, this happens to Professor Maxwell. After debating with himself, he decides that the goals of the humanities should be wisdom and judgment. Wisdom and judgment are certainly good things. It is as hard to quarrel with them as it is (or used to be) to quarrel with motherhood. They recall the ethical values traditionally associated with liberal education. Whether or not they can be measured is beside the point since Professor Maxwell stipulates that the humanities can produce or at least augment them. "It is not denied," he writes, "that reading Chaucer makes one wiser . . . that a detailed knowledge of Bismarck would give our leaders enhanced ability to make decisions on national policy."

The point is that if it is not denied it ought to be. Reading Chaucer's "Miller's Tale" is undoubtedly fun. The reader learns a little about sex in the Middle Ages and a great deal about Chaucer's artistry, but surely he does not come away any wiser than he was before. Conceivably, he may become a little more foolish. By the same token, a biography of Bismarck will teach you something about Germany in the nineteenth century and more than you may want to know about the great Chancellor of Blood and Iron. But your judgment will probably remain unaffected. If it is affected, it may well be for the worse. I am told that Hermann Goering was an avid student of Bismarck. If his reading affected his judgment, it is at least arguable that he would have been better off with "The Miller's Tale."

The demand for simple goals and a pat methodology is a disguised form of the urge of liberal educators and vocationists to put the humanities to some practical use. From the point of view of the humanities themselves, to admit the validity of this impulse is to deny the basic values of humanistic experience—the free play of the mind and its corollary, an expanded sense of the self and its relation to the world. To deny these values would, indeed, be a problem, but it is a problem that disappears as soon as we accept the fact that neither the imagination nor works of imagination can be fitted neatly into the various abstract categories devised to explain them.

VI   The humanities exist because they are native to the human soil. If they were banished today by government decree, they would eventually reappear. In fact, they always are reappearing, Proteus-like, in unexpected forms. The impulse to create large and harmonious forms that is manifested in the Gothic cathedral survives in the twentieth century in Paolo Solari's architectural fantasies. More practically, the universal human need for sculptured form emerges with astonishing force, if not always happy results, in the myriad shapes of the modern automobile, while as legitimate theater becomes a subdominant cultural form, it is replaced by cinema. To paraphrase Horace, if you push Nature out the front door, She comes in at the back.

On the other hand, the fact that the human spirit is resilient does not mean that the contemporary problems of the humanities are trivial. Societies can be life-enhancing or hostile to the free development of the spirit. The difficulties of the humanities within the academy are symptomatic of an illness that pervades modern society. As the role of the humanities in education diminishes, their potential contribution to society diminishes. I mean their potential contribution to the life of each individual and their potential contribution to the culture that is the summation of the lives of all individuals within the society.

CHAPTER 2

The advance of culture continually presents men with new gifts; but the individual sees himself more and more cut off from the enjoyment of them. And what is the good of all this wealth which no single self can ever transmute into its own living possession? Instead of being liberated, is not the individual ego newly burdened by it? In such considerations we first encounter cultural pessimism in its sharpest and most radical formation. . . . the ego no longer draws from culture the consciousness of its own power; it draws only the certainty of its impotence.

Ernst Cassirer, *The Logic of the Humanities*

The unnamable convulsion of our society—the convulsion for which we have no words, no skills, no style of coping—has brought all professional activities into disrepute and even anarchy. We simply do not know whom to train for what contingencies or society, in what numbers, or how.

William Arrowsmith, "Teaching and the Liberal Arts"

THROUGH THE COLLEGE CATALOGUE
WITH SPADE AND CAMERA

ightly understood, a college catalogue is an archeological site. Its system of requirements, its maze of departments, and its lists of courses are frozen history. What looks like chaos to the uninitiated resolves itself in the eye of the cultural historian into a series of strata laid down by a process of intellectual sedimentation that began the year the college was founded. With each new freshet of human knowledge and with each new fashion in educational theory new strata have been deposited. In almost any large institution that is more than half a century old the terrain is enormously rich in anachronisms. They are the intellectual historian's equivalent of the sumptuously decorated skeletons, the engraved blood pitchers, and the polished ceremonial axes retrieved by archeologists from the detritus of particularly depraved primitive tribes.

You have to pick the right school and the right catalogue. By and large the secondary schools and smaller liberal arts colleges have not been able to afford the luxury of deep stratification. A small staff with a frugal budget can innovate, but for everything new that is introduced something old has to go, even if it is only a

31

phrase that existed nowhere but in the mind of the Director of Development. For really exciting digging— layer on layer of fossilized ideas and methods—you need a school with a large endowment (or a generous legislature), a hundred years of history, and an enrollment of ten thousand or more. Insulated by money, tradition, and a constant supply of students, such an institution can afford to carry its past on its shoulders, even though the past is always growing heavier and the institution's balance becomes more and more precarious as it trudges toward the future.

There is a serious point in all this. What is a fascinating stratification to the archeologist of culture may seem quite a different matter to someone who asks what it has to do with the practical realities of education. Growth and variety are healthy when they are controlled. Too much growth and too much variety, however, can be confusing. At a certain point entropy sets in. The curriculum loses coherence. It ceases to be an interrelated group of courses reflecting a conscious educational philosophy and becomes a haphazard list from which students make random choices until they acquire the magic number of credits needed for graduation. When you mix all the colors in a box of water colors, you do not get rainbow-colored water, you get mud-colored water.

Joseph Axelrod, Professor of Education at the University of California at Berkeley, offers the following pessimistic verdict on efforts to establish a coherent curriculum:

The junior college, forfeiting its identity [has] done less than minimally required to meet its major objectives. Four-year colleges, judged by any realistic standard of accomplishment [are] failing. Graduate programs [are] a mish-mash of sense and nonsense which provide . . . for doctoral candidates, in addition to the experience particular to each, the common experience of humiliation.

Harsh words, but not, one feels, entirely without justification, especially as they refer to the humanities curriculum. The organization of the science curriculum is necessarily vertical in part. Some courses have to be taken before others, and this establishes at least a rudimentary structure. The humanities are not organized vertically. At one time students of English or history or philosophy were required to take one course before another, but that time is rapidly passing. Freshmen no longer take survey courses, master the tongues, and read Mark Twain rather than James Joyce. Seminars in *Ulysses* are offered in high school, while Ph.D. candidates sweat over the mysteries of *Tom Sawyer*.

No one, it would seem, can explain why the humanities are organized as they are or what a four-year liberal arts program is supposed to accomplish. Humanities departments are society's chief institutional means for providing students with a sense of human values and of the continuity of culture across the barriers of time and space. If their critics are right, they are doing the reverse. They are demoralizing the men who are supposed to profess them and alienating the students who are their alleged beneficiaries.

This might be regarded as a large and unfortunate accident. In fact, it is not an accident. It was planned. It is the result of careful thought by dedicated, learned, and mostly idealistic men.

Rather than speak in the abstract I will take a specific example. I will use a group of catalogues issued by a real institution, which I will call College X, between 1967 and 1971. Since I am more familiar with English department offerings than the offerings of other humanities departments, I will concentrate on these. College X is a state institution more than a century old. It enrolls over 15,000 students. About 700 are undergraduate English majors and about 300 are working toward graduate degrees in English. In addition, some 3,000 freshmen and sophomores annually take required English courses in composition and literature. I emphasize that I have not chosen College X because it provides especially dire examples of curricular entropy. Quite the contrary, it is by all standards a first-rate school with an outstanding English department. The catalogue of almost any other institution of the same size would offer equally instructive examples. I also recognize that a catalogue is an exercise in wish-fulfillment. It gives someone's Platonic idea of what the college does and the reality is usually as far from the idea as the shadows on Plato's cave are from the objects that produced them. For better or for worse, however, the catalogue is the record you have to work with if you want to talk about the curriculum.

According to my catalogues, between 1967 and 1971 the English department at College X offered an average of seventy-eight undergraduate courses per year, sixty-five of them for junior and senior English majors. The preamble to the course listing carries the information that a major can take no fewer than six and no more than eight courses from the junior-senior group. Eight courses, that is, out of sixty-five. It seems reasonable to ask why a student needs such a bewildering range of choice. Is the subject of English really that vast? Can it not be compressed or shaped so that a conscientious student has at least a glimmering hope of sampling its major areas?

At best the arrangement is inefficient. In practice it is a pedagogic disaster. Eight choices out of twenty might conceivably impress a student with the notion that life is brief and art is long. But eight choices out of sixty-five is a different matter. It begets despair. It leaves the student morosely dabbling in the rime-cold sea of a vast, formless collection of courses. When he has summoned his courage and made his eight choices he remains aware that he has opted not to take fifty-seven others. What has he missed? Moreover, the chances are that no matter how craftily he has plotted his strategy, the courses he does take will be disparate in subject and approach. Few of them will relate to any of the others, much less to the courses he takes outside of the English department. The situation is so patently absurd that it raises the question of whether the English curriculum exists at all—of whether there is a body of knowledge that the professionals agree is essential to a well-rounded knowledge of English literature and that students should reasonably be expected to master, or at least encounter, if they aspire to be labeled "Bachelor of Arts in English."

At the same time, as I have already remarked, the course list is not accidental. Appearances to the contrary, it is the work of trained men, genuinely dedicated to their profession, who have discussed each course many times in committee and who have usually registered their opinions by procedures as democratic as those of the fabled New England town-hall meetings. You can ridicule them and impugn their motives, but if you do this you are committing an injustice. Lobbying for special interests goes on in the academy as everywhere else, but the real problem is that decisions about individual courses are made individually, one by one. The curriculum is often affectionately criticized, much as you might give an old dog an affectionate slap on the backside for committing an impropriety on the living room carpet, but it is seldom examined from the point of view of its relation to the idea of educating students and never—well, hardly ever—revised from this point of view.

This leads to my first observation about the humanities curriculum. It has a prodigious capacity for growth and almost no inclination whatsoever to shrink. As new fashions, interests, and theories appear in society, they are packaged in courses and listed as departmental offerings. The reverse is not true. Old courses survive. Many of them flourish. Even when the fashions that produced them are discredited, they are passed from generation to generation like family heirlooms that nobody likes but everybody would feel guilty about throwing away. John C. Gerber, veteran chairman of a large and proud English department in the Midwest, makes the point in The *Bulletin* of the Association of Departments of English of May 1970:

As a profession we have possessed an unholy obsession with courses. This obsession has nurtured the conviction that everything a student should learn, or even wishes to learn, should be covered by a course. In the 1930's we began to develop courses that covered every conceivable aspect of English and American literature from, as the cliché has it, Beowulf to Virginia Woolf. Subsequently, each new school of literary criticism brought its own clutch of courses, and so did such programs as linguistics, comparative literature, American studies, and creative writing. More recently, we have added courses in contemporary literature, folklore, bibliographical analysis, and black literature. And the end is nowhere near in sight. Note that courses always get added, almost never dropped or telescoped or enlarged.

Sedimentation begins at any institution on the day when it is founded. At College X, the earliest stratum represents local adaptation during the nineteenth century of the educational theory of the Renaissance. Actually, the roots of the theory extend to classical times, since Renaissance educators did not think of themselves as innovators so much as reformers clearing

II

away the debris of medieval ignorance by reviving the great traditions of Greece and Rome.

The ideal shared by classical and Renaissance educators was expressed in a phrase by the elder Cato: *vir bonus dicendi peritus*—the good man skilled in public speaking. Commenting on this ideal, Quintilian, perhaps the most influential theorist of education from the first century A.D. to the nineteenth century, explained in *The Education of the Orator:*

> It is no hack-advocate, no hireling phoebe, nor yet, to use a harsher term, a serviceable attorney of the class generally known as *causidici*, that I am seeking to form, but a man who has added to extraordinary natural gifts a thorough mastery of all the fairest departments of knowledge. . . . Only a small portion of all these abilities will be required for the defense of the innocent, the repression of crime or the support of truth against falsehood in suits involving money. It is true that our supreme orator will bear his part in such tasks, but his powers will be displayed with brighter splendor in greater matters than these, when he is called to direct the counsels of the senate and guide the people from the paths of error into better things.

Today we would describe this as a program to train a professional elite. Students are to be selected on the basis of conspicuous natural talent. They are to be given a comprehensive general education with the emphasis on the liberal arts—philosophy, history, and literature. The curriculum has two aims: to provide character training so that the students will meet the first requirement (goodness) of Cato's formula, and to equip them with the skills, especially skill in public speaking, needed for administration. On completing their education they will take their place in the bureaucracy as lawyers, magistrates, civil servants, and legislators, and the most successful will be the leaders of the future. The system is a blueprint for maintaining an establishment. If it sounds familiar it should. It is a blueprint that was followed, by and large, in the major universities in England and the United States until after World War II.

Quintilian's program is based on what modern educators would call the theory of communication. Classical writers equated communication with oratory, and the title of Quintilian's treatise is *The Education of the Orator*. The theory of communication had been elaborately codified under the term rhetoric. Reduced to standard manuals which are recognizable ancestors of modern textbooks in English composition, rhetoric was the central discipline of the Greek and Roman schools. It embraced written as well as spoken communication. During the Christian era the status of rhetoric was enhanced by a new and extremely important kind of oratory, preaching. Medieval theorists placed rhetoric second, between grammar and logic, in the trivium of basic curriculum subjects, while Renaissance humanists prided themselves on having restored it to its ancient supremacy. The age of print did not dethrone rhetoric; it merely caused a shift in emphasis from spoken to written communication.

The rhetorical curriculum had three components. First, it involved the theory of rhetoric, from the effective use of sentence structure and imagery to methods of organization to techniques of logical and affective argument. Second, it required extensive readings in works considered literary and philosophical master-pieces. While students could become familiar with the liberal arts through these readings, their primary function was to provide examples of persuasive, elegant, and morally uplifting expression. Third, the rhetorical curriculum emphasized practice. It provided for regular exercises in composition and public speaking based on standard forms called *suasoriae* and *controversiae*.

At College X the most primitive stratum of the English curriculum is a layer of courses in rhetoric and public speaking. Rhetoric has been renamed English Composition. Two courses in composition are required of all freshmen except those exempted by advanced placement tests. The content of the composition courses has varied over the years, but in 1967, the year of the earliest of my catalogues, the first semester consisted of the principles of grammar and rhetoric, readings in an anthology of essays chosen to illustrate writing techniques, and weekly theme assignments. The second semester concentrated on logic, argumentation, and methods of proof and required a long term paper in addition to shorter assignments. Beyond the freshman requirement the catalogue lists seven courses in writing and no fewer than twelve courses in public speaking. These include Advanced Expository Writing ("effective organization and presentation of information and ideas . . . communicating information, explaining ideas"), Business Writing ("communicative factors"), Scientific

Writing ("to aid the scientist in the communication situations of his professional career"), American Public Address, and Advanced Public Speaking.

From the sixteenth through the eighteenth century, the literature that students read to learn eloquence was almost exclusively Greek and Latin. As late as the 1950s many American colleges still required two years of Latin for admission. Long before this, however, modern languages had supplanted the classics. As far as the rhetorical curriculum was concerned, the classics had ceased to be useful models for speaking and writing. If you speak and write in English, your best models will be in English. Educators heroically resisted this simple truth, but even educators must eventually come to terms with the obvious. Moreover, the literary part of rhetoric had always tended to outgrow the confines of the rhetorical curriculum. This tendency was equally strong whether the students read ancient or modern masterpieces. No matter how hard you concentrate on asyndeton and paronomasia in Vergil's *Aeneid* or striking maxims in Shakespeare's *Julius Caesar* or techniques of description in Fielding's *Tom Jones* it is hard not to be seduced into considering these works as literature as well as examples of eloquence.

In the nineteenth century the claim of literature to separate and equal status was recognized. Curricular mitosis occurred and independent departments of classical and vernacular literature were established. When this

III

happened, the new programs were shaped by several influences. First, there was historical precedent. Cato's formula has two parts. If literary studies are separated from rhetoric, it can still be argued that they have a moral influence on students. Reading Homer or Cervantes or Shakespeare can be justified as character training. Puzzling through optatives and pluperfect subjunctives can be said to encourage mental discipline, while the high seriousness of the *Iliad* or *Hamlet* or *Hermann und Dorothea* can provide the great thoughts needed by future leaders. By and large, this line of argument was favored by classicists and academic conservatives like Sainte-Beuve and Matthew Arnold. It was taken over ready-made from rhetoric and it had the virtue of emphasizing the social value of literary studies.

A quite different influence was exerted by advocates of specialized approaches to literature that have nothing to do with rhetoric. Some of these approaches are as old as the Greeks; others emerged during the Renaissance and later as corollaries of the effort to produce sound, well-annotated editions of ancient and modern authors. Palaeography, epigraphy, archeology, and comparative grammar are cases in point. They can be grouped loosely under the label of philology. The Germans were the first to make philology a formal, articulated program in the curriculum. They prided themselves on having changed literary study from a haphazard mixture of rhetoric and impressionism into an exact science—a *Strengwissenschaft*. Philology provided subject matter for the emerging departments of literature, but it did so at the expense of creating a gulf between those educators who still wanted to produce good men skilled in speaking and those who wanted to produce literary scientists.

Whatever the merits of the two positions, the decisive factor in shaping departments of modern literature was nationalism. I do not mean the generalized patriotism that is as old as Homer, but the theory of the nature and destiny of the national state formulated by the German Romantics. For the humanities, and especially for literature, the essential concept was the idea that each nation has a unique quality—a *Volksgeist*—and that the unity and progress of the nation depends on cultivation of this quality. In spite of the fact that most national populations are ethnically mixed, the concept of the *Volksgeist* was frequently equated with the theory that each race has innate psychological characteristics, and given the climate of thought in the nineteenth century, this unquestionably added to its attractions.

The prophet of the *Volksgeist* was Johann Gottfried von Herder. Herder's influence, particularly as deepened and sophisticated in Hegel's dialectic, extends across the entire nineteenth century. What Herder taught—and what was soon accepted as gospel in the academy—was that the purest manifestation of the *Volksgeist* occurs in works of art, especially in works of literature. Furthermore, if you are looking for the *Volksgeist* in its purest form, you are most likely to find it in the earliest literature of each nation, where it is uncontaminated by foreign influences. For modern nations this means medieval literature. Accordingly, the Germans sought their *Volksgeist* in the *Nibelungenlied*, in folk songs and ballads, and in the romances of Gottfried von Strassburg and the lyrics of Walther von der Vogelweide. The French looked to *The Song of Roland*, the Italians to *The Divine Comedy*, the Spanish to the ballads of the Cid, and the English to *Beowulf.* Theoretically, after the *Volksgeist* has been identified in early works, it can then be traced through the literature of more sophisticated ages. The classic example of the application of this theory is Hippolyte Taine's *History of English Literature*, published in 1864. Taine uses the term "race" rather than *Volksgeist*. It refers to qualities allegedly innate to the Anglo-Saxon mind. In the *History* race is a constant. After defining it through a discussion of Anglo-Saxon writing, Taine traces it through the later periods of English literature up to the Victorian period, taking due account, of course, of the general leavening of the English racial spirit that occurred in the wake of the Norman Conquest. To explain the fact that race takes on different colorations in different writers, Taine suggested that it is modified in any specific work by the variables of "moment" and "milieu."

Once the academy discovered the *Volksgeist*, simple patriotism demanded that courses on the various national literatures be added to those on the classics. Because learning about the *Volksgeist* required a heavy dose of medieval literature, there was a happy marriage of interests between the nationalists and the philologists. The Germans had invented the *Volksgeist* and *Strengwissenschaft* in the first place. Accordingly, they proceeded to establish full-scale programs in literary history and philology. Students labored through courses in Germanic philology, Romance philology, Gothic, Old Norse, Middle High German, Old English, comparative linguistics, and the editing of manuscripts, the latter eventually gaining the status of an industry with the founding of national editing factories on the model of the *École des Chartes*. Although the naive observer might assume that post-medieval authors like Shakespeare and Alexander Pope could be approached without the ponderous apparatus of *Strengwissenschaft*, scholars on both sides of the Atlantic soon dispelled that illusion. What later writers lacked in linguistic challenge was offset by studies in text, sources, influence, biography, and historical backgrounds.

The first graduate program on the German model was established at Johns Hopkins University in 1876 and soon spread to such major universities as Chicago, Cornell, Harvard, Columbia, Michigan, and Wisconsin. By 1876 the study of vernacular literature had become as technical, as specialized, and as remote from the normal interests of mankind as the study of the classics. As the Hopkins program took hold, undergraduate programs were revised to conform to what was happening in the graduate schools. The difference was that undergraduates were considered a mixed bag—certainly less dedicated and probably less intelligent than graduate students. While graduates wrestled with Middle High German and *Beowulf*, undergraduates were given the easier centuries from Shakespeare to Matthew Arnold. Graduates pondered the Great Vowel Shift in seminars; undergraduates were treated to lectures on the sources of the *Faerie Queene*, preromantic elements in James Thomson's *The Seasons*, and the influence of Milton on Wordsworth's blank verse. As a concession to undergraduate superficiality, lecturers occasionally digressed from *Strengwissenschaft* into comments on the ethical and aesthetic values of the works themselves.

These details are worth recalling because the stratum that follows the earliest, rhetorical layer at College X consists of two groups of courses: a group arranged chronologically from the earliest to the most recent literary periods, and a second group dealing with linguistics and grammar. The first invites students to trace the path of English literature from infancy to maturity. The second is fallout from graduate studies. It provides a smattering of philology for those who will not continue to graduate school.

The most obvious courses from this era are the period surveys. The English major can take courses in The Middle Ages, The Renaissance, The Seventeenth Century, The Neo-Classic Period, The Romantic Period, The Victorian Period, The Age of Transition, and Modern English Literature. Parallel courses are offered in American literature beginning with Colonial Literature, reminding us that the discovery of an English *Volksgeist* led in the fullness of time to the discovery of an American *Volksgeist*. In all, sixteen period surveys are offered to undergraduates. These are supplemented by special courses on Chaucer, Shakespeare, and Milton. Old English is not offered to undergraduates, but philology is present in this stratum in three courses: English Grammar ("modern English grammar—traditional, structural, and transfunctional"), The History of the English Language ("its historical background and development"), and Modern English.

Note that the rhetorical tradition was not crowded out by *Strengwissenschaft* and the *Volksgeist*. The newer courses were simply *added to* the older ones. The result was a curriculum involving three distinct educational goals: the creation of good men skilled in speaking, the study of the English *Volksgeist*, and the acquisition of specialized linguistic knowledge.

IV

Even so, the curriculum has the merit of being relatively simple. It is at least comprehensible in its outline. It was challenged aggressively between 1910 and 1930. In the United States the principal spokesman for the opposition was Irving Babbitt, a professor of literature at Harvard. In *Literature and the American College* (1908), Babbit lamented the professionalizing of the classics:

It is to be accounted one of the chief disasters to our higher culture that our classical teachers as a body have fallen so far short ... that they have come instead entirely under the influence of the narrowest school of German philology.

The modern languages, he felt, were no better served:

We should at least insist that the college teacher of ancient or modern literature be something more than a mere specialist. To regard a man as qualified for a college position in these subjects merely because he has investigated some minute point of linguistics or literary history—this is, to speak plainly, preposterous.

As for the tendency to concentrate on medieval literature:

The great danger of the whole class of philologists we are discussing is to substitute literary history for literature itself—a danger that has been especially manifest in a field where literary phenomena are numerous and genuine literature comparatively scarce, that of the Middle Ages. ... The vital question, after all, is not whether one *chanson de geste* is derived from another *chanson de geste*, but whether either work has any claim to the attention of a serious person.

Babbitt also commented wryly on the division in the English curriculum between the rhetors and the philologists:

At one extreme of the average English department is the philological medievalist, who is grounded in Gothic and Old Norse and Anglo-Saxon; at the other extreme is the dilettante, who gives courses in "daily themes," and, like the sophists of old, instructs ingenuous youth in the art of expressing itself before it has anything to express.

Babbitt's solution was to reject *Strengwissenschaft* in favor of comparative literature. Comparative literature, he believed, would permit students to read masterpieces and skip the second rate. Most important—and here we come to the heart of Babbitt's position—reading the masterpieces would expose the student to an "unbroken chain of literary and intellectual tradition which extends from the ancient to the modern world." The tradition that Babbitt had in mind is quite specific. It is an ethical tradition that Babbitt called "the humane standard" and that he discovered in all the true masterpieces from Confucius to Goethe:

Now the humane standard may be gained by a few through philosophic insight, but in most cases it will be attained, if at all, by a knowledge of good literature—by a familiarity with that golden chain of masterpieces which links together into a single tradition the more permanent experience of the race; books which so agree in essentials that they seem, as Emerson puts it, to be the work of one all-seeing all-hearing gentleman.

As should be evident, we are back on familiar ground. What Babbitt is offering, and what comparative literature was supposed to produce, is Cato's good man skilled in speaking, with the emphasis on goodness. The larger objective is also familiar. It is to produce leaders. As Babbitt wrote in *Rousseau and Romanticism*:

The design of higher education, so far as it deserves the name, is to produce leaders, and on the quality of the leadership must depend more than on any other single factor, the success or failure of democracy.

Babbitt called his movement "New Humanism." It spread from Harvard to Princeton, where it was promulgated by Paul Elmer Moore, then throughout the Ivy League and its imitators among state colleges and universities. As we have seen, College X began by stressing rhetoric, philology, and literary history. For many years its required sophomore English course was a perfectly standard example of the historical approach. It was a two-semester survey beginning with Old English authors (in translation) and continuing through the twentieth century. From *Beowulf* to *Virginia Woolf* as the cliché has it. Under the impact of the New Humanism the first-semester survey was altered drastically. The "second-rate" authors were dropped, and the subject matter was limited to readings in three authentic first-raters—Chaucer, Shakespeare, and Milton. Some time after this revision occurred, the requirement of a second semester of English literature was abolished for reasons unrelated to New Humanism. The second-semester course survives as an elective. The number of authors treated has been reduced and the emphasis is on masterpieces, but the historical tradition still shows through the New Humanist overlay. For an unambiguous example of the influence of the New Humanism we can turn to the sophomore honors course, which promises readings in world (as against English) masterpieces: *The Odyssey*, *Oedipus Rex*, *King Lear*, and *Hedda Gabler*.

Although the concepts and attitudes of New Humanism appear frequently in upper-division English courses at College X and frequently determine the shape of special sections and honors seminars, there are few course descriptions that emphasize this fact. The reason is simple. During the period when the New Humanism flourished, the English Department at College X was self-consciously Germanic. Its professors opposed the New Humanism on three grounds: its didacticism, the lack of focus implicit in the very broad scope of its concept of literary classics, and the superficiality involved in the comparative treatment, out of historical context and frequently in translation, of masterpieces of different ages and cultures. The principal deposit left by New Humanism at College X is the college's program in comparative literature, which was originally sponsored by the foreign language departments rather than the English department. Although the English department now cooperates in this program, its continuing skepticism is illustrated by the fact that after some thirty years in the catalogue comparative literature is still a program. It has never managed to become a department.

During the 1930s both historical scholarship and New V Humanism were challenged by a movement known as the New Criticism. The chief names associated with this movement are I. A. Richards, William Empson, John Crowe Ransom, Allen Tate, and Cleanth Brooks. The New Critics attacked Germanicism and New Humanism with equal vehemence. Germanic scholarship, they argued, makes literary studies into a mindless pursuit of facts at the expense of art. The New Humanism, on the other hand, substitutes moral pomposities for the experience of the thing itself. It is clear that the thrust of the New Criticism was basically aesthetic in spite of differences among members of the movement. The chief historical influence on the movement was Samuel Taylor Coleridge with more proximate influences from Poe, "art for art's sake," Benedetto Croce, and the method of close literary analysis used in France called *explication de texte*. For the most part, the New Critics rejected historical and biographical information as irrelevant—sometimes positively misleading—in literary studies. They advocated courses based on close reading of a limited number of works in their original languages.

Evidently the New Critics spoke for a great many teachers and students. After the publication in 1938 of *Understanding Poetry* by Cleanth Brooks and Robert Penn Warren, the New Criticism became a major, if not a dominant movement in the teaching of literature. It remained so until its influence began to wane, around 1965.

The deposits of the New Criticism at College X are Introduction to Poetry ("narrative, dramatic, and lyric poems as aesthetic processes"), Types of Literature ("a continuing study of literary forms"), and Interpretation of Poetry. Two of these courses use (or used) the Brooks and Warren text. Other, less obvious accretions from the New Critics are Introduction to Fiction ("a close study of . . . short stories and short works of fiction with emphasis on technical problems which the writer has solved") and two courses in criticism. The courses in criticism are not wholly "new critical" but were stimulated by the interest of the New Critics in the theory of literature. Critical Approaches to Literature promises "illustration of major perspectives such as historical, formal, moral, myths, 'New Critical', philosophical, psychological, or sociological," while Principles of Literary Art offers a historical survey of major critical theories from Aristotle to the twentieth century.

This accumulation of strata might seem to exhaust all possibilities. It does not. For example, the catalogue lists a large group of courses that approach literature in terms of genres. These courses are hard to date but some of them are venerable. The first English courses using the genre approach were introduced in the late nineteenth century. They were courses in folklore (a corollary of the search for the *Volksgeist*) and in drama. Both types of course involved much discussion of the theory of genres (What is a ballad? What is the difference between a ceremony and a drama?), and the drama courses flourished because of the centrality of Shakespeare and contemporaries like Christopher Marlowe and Ben Jonson in English literature.

The theory of genres was sufficiently well established by the turn of the century to cause Benedetto Croce to attack it as "the chief intellectualist heresy" in his *Aesthetic* (1901). Croce complained that literary genres are procrustean beds and that works should be judged on the basis of what they are rather than whether or not they fit an arbitrary formula. In spite of Croce, genre studies flourished. College X offers eight courses on drama, including the inevitable course on Shakespeare, seven courses on prose fiction, and four courses on poetry, which, however, involve New Critical as well as genre concepts. In addition, there is a course on the English Ballad, and two courses are crosslisted with the Folklore curriculum—British and American Folk Song and Folk Narrative.

At this point we reach the most recent strata. After World War II several things happened to the curriculum. As writers kept writing, the body of literature kept growing. This resulted in the addition of courses to the historical sequence. Contemporary literature of the Joyce, Yeats, and Eliot period was an early arrival, and as demands for relevance multiplied, courses were devised for the period after World War II. Some of the newer courses are general (A Survey of Twentieth-Century British and American Literature). Others show the influence of the genre approach: British and American Fiction since World War II; English and American Drama of the Twentieth Century; and Twentieth-Century Poetry. Recent interest in popular culture is reflected in Movie Criticism, while the discovery of an American *Volksgeist* has led inevitably to regional and ethnic *Volksgeists*. Hence courses on the Literature of the X Region and American Negro Literature.

This is not all. College X has long prided itself on its hospitality to the creative spirit. During the sixties this spirit flourished. A rudimentary program in creative writing expanded to five courses subdivided into the writing of fiction and the writing of poetry (the influence of the genre approach). At the same time, in response to demands for creative course design, College X added a group of self-consciously innovative seminars, honors courses, and courses so fluid they can be described in the catalogue only as Studies in Literary Topics and Directed Readings in Literature.

We are now on top of the strata that comprise the English curriculum of College X. To our consternation or joy as the case may be, sedimentation continues. As I mentioned, within the last few years courses have been added in regional and Negro literature (new *Volksgeists*), literature since World War II (a new period), movies (a new genre), and "literary topics" (a new something). Dazzling opportunities lie ahead. American Indian Literature, Hebrew Literature (subdivided into Sephardic and Ashkenazi), Chicano Literature, and American-Oriental Literature all have *Volksgeists* that cry out for exploration. The Literature of Women is already flourishing on many campuses and will doubtless soon appear at College X, with exciting possibilities for division by period, genre, region, and ethnic group. Only a Polonius could do justice to such future offerings as Nineteenth Century Black Female Fiction or Modern Lyric Poetry by Northeastern Puerto Rican Males. Considering the richness of the subject, teachers of movie courses can hardly be expected to rest content with a single anemic survey. The yet unknowing world awaits movie courses by the decade (the silent twenties, the talking thirties, the colorful forties), by the genre (romance, thriller, western, musical), and on the comparative model (Studies in Eisenstein, Bergman, and Billy Wilder). In the fullness of time there will doubtless be enough lady directors to justify. . . .

VI But enough. Plainly the mass grows before our very eyes. Rhetoric, philology, historicism, humanism, aestheticism, genre theory, modernism, ethnicism, social engagement, and psychological experiment—they are all there. No voice is wholly lost and the result is like the Tower of Babel. If this is a baffling situation for the student, if it seems to represent an abdication of the responsibility of professionals to understand what they are professing and to present its central elements in a coherent form, the English Department of College X can honestly answer its critics as Martin Luther answered his Catholic adversaries: "Here I stand, I cannot do otherwise."

But even though the present curriculum may have been historically inevitable, I think we have to admit that it is absurd. Dropping out is as popular on the campus as free flicks, while those who persevere to graduation are usually deeply confused about what they learned. If you ask a recent graduate at an alumni reunion what he got out of his humanities courses, chances are he will ponder a moment, shrug his shoulders, and head back to the bar. If not—if he is one of those who truly cares about education—you may be in for a stormy session revolving around the idea that if the curriculum fails to add up, the academy itself has failed.

But this is too harsh. To review the history of the curriculum is to be reminded that it has been shaped by the sensitivity of humanists to vital currents in the surrounding culture, not indifference. If the humanities curriculum is a tangle of contradictory traditions, so is the culture from which the traditions were drawn. On the other hand, the academy has clearly reached the point where it must do more than bundle what comes to it from the outside into packages called courses and add them to the catalogue. If humanists cannot arrive at a unified understanding of what they are doing, the humanities and the humanistic component in education risk being discredited.

There is evidence that humanists are aware of this and trying with varying degrees of success to do something about it. Instead of commenting on their efforts, I will end with an image intended as an emblem of the situation I have described in the preceding pages. It is the image of a literary archaeologist, spade and camera in hand, standing over an imposing mound of sediment labeled "the humanities curriculum." If the record he brings to light is depressing, it is also, to quote Nietzsche, human, all too human.

CHAPTER 3

It was culture itself that gave these wounds to modern humanity. The inner union of human nature was broken, and a destructive contest divided its harmonious forces directly; on the one hand an enlarged experience and a more distinct thinking necessitated a sharper separation of the sciences, while on the other hand the more sophisticated machinery of states necessitated a stricter sundering of ranks and occupations.

Schiller, *Letters on the Aesthetic Education of Man*

Up to the time of Kant a philosophy of beauty always meant an attempt to reduce our aesthetic experience to an alien principle and to an alien jurisdiction. Kant in his *Critique of Judgment* was the first to give clear and convincing proof of the autonomy of art. All former systems had looked for a principle of art within the sphere either of theoretical knowledge or the moral life.

Ernst Cassirer, *An Essay on Man*

THE ORATOR AND THE POET:
THE DILEMMA OF
RENAISSANCE HUMANISM

f a general failure of nerve and a disintegrating curriculum are the outward and visible signs of the plight of the humanities, the causes of the sickness go much deeper. They are rooted, I believe, in a fundamental ambivalence about what the humanities should be. This ambivalence goes back to the classical period, but it became apparent during the Renaissance. The revival of classical ideals at the end of the Middle Ages was part of a general movement for practical social reform. Inevitably, however, it had a nonutilitarian dimension. That is, at the same time that the Renaissance humanists advocated a philosophy based on *praxis*—action—the subject matter of their curriculum encouraged *gnosis*—knowing, or contemplation.

The tension between *praxis* and *gnosis* is a recurrent theme in humanist writing and the experience of the humanists themselves. Humanist theory sought an accommodation—ideally, a fusion. What the humanists learned from their experience was that the combination does not work. The demands of the practical world are different from those of art. This is an important fact because the tendency of industrial society has been constantly to widen the division between *praxis* and

61

gnosis, while our official explanations of liberal education and the importance of the humanities in culture still echo the Renaissance commonplaces.

Rather than talk about the problem in general terms, I will concentrate on two figures who typify Renaissance ideals: the orator who is entrusted with the Ciceronian mission of ordering and directing society, and the poet, who shares the Ciceronian mission according to Renaissance theory, but whose attempts to carry out this mission in real life led to dissatisfaction and even bitter disillusionment with the possibilities of social reform, and to the development of an aesthetic that was finally given self-conscious expression at the end of the eighteenth century.

II   I will begin with an image rather than a text. The image is that of Francis Petrarch standing in the Senatorial Palace on Rome's Capitoline Hill on April 8, 1341. He is wearing the ceremonial robe of King Robert of Naples, and he has just been crowned with the laurel—the first such coronation in Rome, it is said, for 1,000 years.

In the oration which he delivers after being crowned, Petrarch speaks of the love that draws him up the lonely and difficult slopes of Parnassus, and of the stimulus that his wish to advance the honor of the state provides for the ascent. At this point my scene is an emblem of the relationship between beauty and power as complementary means of human betterment—between the laurel of Apollo and the robe of King Robert; the lonely slopes of Parnassus and the civic glory of Italy.

In deference to Petrarch, who is a poet delivering an oration in the Capitoline Palace, I will speak of it as a relationship between the orator and the poet in the typical roles assigned them by humanist rhetorical theory. That is to say, a relationship between the ideal leader who uses language to persuade, and the ideal artist who uses language to reveal what Petrarch, in his oration, calls "an inner force divinely infused in the poet's spirit."

As for the first role, the role of the ideal leader, we are repeatedly told by humanists that their objective is nothing less than the reform of human society. The revival of antiquity was not a game played out for the delectation of scholars; it was a means to a political end. The same concern for political ends is evident throughout the Renaissance in the popularity of imaginary states like Utopia, of the pastoral never-never land of Corydon and Phyllis, of manuals on the education of princes, of programs for the founding of model schools, of courtesy books, and, on occasion, of grandiose projects to transform society root and branch, from the Sacred Republic of Cola di Rienzo to the Protectorate of Oliver Cromwell. Time and again, too, we encounter complementary efforts by artists to lift rather sordid political realities to the level of the ideal—in Verrocchio's equestrian statue of Bartolommeo Colleoni, in Holbein's portraits of Francis I and Henry VIII, in Michelangelo's tomb portraits of Lorenzo and Giuliano de'Medici. If there is a tension in these works—a touch of cruelty in the grace of Colleoni, of cynicism in the smile of Francis I, of disillusionment with the world's vanities in the anguished figures symbolizing time over which Lorenzo and Giuliano are seated—this tension is a measure of the distance between things as they ought to be and things as they are. After the revival of Aristotle's *Poetics* in the sixteenth century it was generally accepted that by depicting things as they ought to be, the artist contributed to the improvement of things as they are.

In the grand scheme of reform, the orator occupied the central position. As any Renaissance schoolboy could tell you, Demosthenes was the main pillar of Athenian liberty and Cicero gained eternal glory by his defense of the Roman Republic. Impatient with the chop-logic, the jargon, and the endless theorizing of the medieval scholastics, the humanists looked to the orator to change society and made rhetoric, which is training for oratory, the central discipline of their educational system. How, in fact, do you translate the morality of Christ and the ethics of Socrates into social realities? Not through ever more obscure treatises written by professors for other professors, the argument ran, but through addressing mankind at large. In theory, at least, the orator is trained for just this mission. Whether he speaks in the public forum or the assembly or the law court or from the pulpit, his announced object is persuasion and his instrument is eloquence. Here is a typical comment—typical even in its fine Italian condescension—from a letter by Aeneas Silvius to his friend Adam Mulin in farthest England:

I read your letter with great eagerness and was amazed that Latin style had penetrated even into Britain. It is true that there have been some few Englishmen who have cultivated the eloquence of Cicero. . . . Persevere, therefore, friend Adam. Hold fast and increase the eloquence you possess. Consider it the most honorable thing possible to excel your fellows in that whereby men excel the other living creatures. Great is eloquence. Nothing so much rules the world. Political action is the result of persuasion; his opinion prevails with the people who best knows how to persuade.

Eloquence, that is, is the power to shape society: "nothing so much rules the world." The curious emblem of Hercules with chains in his tongue makes the same point. Alexander Ross explains the emblem in his book *Mystagogus Poeticus*:

By Hercules the ancients did not only mean valor and strength of body, but the force of eloquence also—which they did express by that picture of Hercules clothed in a horse skin, armed with a club, with bow and arrows, having small chains proceeding from his tongue and tied to the ears of people whom he drew after him: By which they signified how sharp and powerful eloquence is to pierce and subdue the affections of people and draw them far.

If the image of people being led by chains tied to their ears makes the idea of power associated with oratory uncomfortably obvious, we have the assurance of the humanists that it is all in a good cause. The end in view is the improvement of mankind, and if men have to be dragged to the Good Life in chains, then so be it. Cato's requirement for the orator is that he be a *vir bonus dicendi peritus*—a good man skilled in speaking—and the emphasis is on the first phrase—the *vir bonus*; while Crassus, who speaks for the divine Tully in the *De Oratore*, insists that whatever else he may or may not know, the orator should be thoroughly versed in moral philosophy.

As a result of the Christian dispensation, Renaissance humanists could claim a sanction far more authoritative than Cato. The title of Thomas Wilson's preface to his *Art of Rhetoric* reads "Eloquence first given by God, and after lost by man, and at last repaired by God again." Eloquence, Wilson explains, was the first cause of human civilization, and the earliest orators were instruments of divine will:

Whereas men lived brutishly in open fields, having neither house to shroud them in, nor attire to clothe their bodies, nor yet any regard to see their best avail, these [early leaders] appointed by God called them together by utterance of speech and persuaded with them what was good, what was bad, and what was gainful for mankind. And . . . being somewhat drawn with the pleasantness of reason, and the sweetness of utterance, after a certain space they became . . . of wild, sober; of cruel, gentle; of fools, wise; of beasts, men—such force hath the tongue, and such is the power of Eloquence and Reason, that most men are forced, even to yield in that which most standeth against their will.

Like Aeneas Silvius, Wilson considers eloquence a source of power. It is psychological rather than physical power, but it is power nonetheless, for it causes men "even to yield in that which most standeth against their will." Wilson adds the rhetorical question, "What man would not rather look to rule like a lord than to live like an underling—if by reason he were not persuaded . . . to live in his own vocation." The ability to persuade is the ability to force men to act against their own natural inclinations. Although invisible, the chains are still there.

But it is all in a good cause. No humanist can doubt this without questioning the validity of humanism itself. The orator is a good man, perhaps even an instrument of God. He civilizes, orders, upholds justice, and, from the pulpit, leads (or drags) his followers along the road to salvation. The figure of the evil orator, whose tongue drops manna and can make the worse appear the better part, was familiar to the Renaissance—we need look no further than Shakespeare's Richard III or Milton's Satan—but the evil orator was considered the exception, not the rule. The remedy, as Ben Jonson solemnly explained, is for the good man, the *vir bonus*, to study rhetoric as assiduously as the bad man. Rhetorical skills being equal, the orator with truth on his side is certain to prevail.

But I began with the image of a poet delivering an oration, and so far I have said little about poetry. My emblem of Petrarch on the Capitoline Hill suggests that the poet is so closely related to the orator in Renaissance thought that the two can easily merge into a single figure. In fact, the orator and the poet had already been closely associated in the classical past to which the Renaissance looked for guidance. The topic "Is Vergil to be considered an orator or a poet?" was a set piece for late classical exercises in composition called *controversiae*; while a lengthy section of the *Saturnalia*, a fourth-century work by Macrobius, ploddingly defends the idea that Vergil is not only an orator but a supreme orator. As we know, the practice of reading the poets in the schools to cull images and aphorisms for the improvement of prose style was standard in the classical curriculum long before it was advocated by Renaissance educators.

Images and aphorisms aside, however, the main point and chief Renaissance justification for poetry is that the poet shares the political mission of the orator. In the *Pro Archia Poeta* Cicero explains how Ennius celebrated the Roman people and Roman ideals; and Vergil's *Aeneid* is a case study of the way that poetry can be used to celebrate the state and its ruling class. The difference between oratory and poetry is not one of function but degree. Coluccio Salutati, disciple of Petrarch and Chancellor of Florence, makes this point very clear. After defining the orator in the approved Catonian fashion as a *vir bonus dicendi peritus*, he defines the poet as a *vir optimus laudandi vituperandique peritus*—a perfect man skilled in praise and blame. Poetry, in other words, is a higher form of oratory. It is eloquence, and it is a supreme eloquence.

Given this attitude, it is not surprising to find that exactly the same claims made for oratory are made for poetry. If the orator can be considered a founder of civilized society, so can the poet and on much better evidence. The achievements of the *prisci poetae*—the poets of the earliest period of human history—fascinated Renaissance critics. They are celebrated at the very beginning of the Renaissance by Boccaccio in Books XIV and XV of *The Genealogy of the Gods*, and again a century later by Politian in his poem *Nutricia*, in which poetry is described as the nurse of human civilization. A century later the commonplaces were neatly summarized for Englishmen in *The Art of English Poesie*, ascribed to George Puttenham:

Poetry was the original cause and occasion of [men's] first assemblies; when before, the people remained . . . dispersed like the wild beasts, lawless and naked . . . so as they little differed for their manner of life from the very brutes of the field. Whereupon it is feigned that Amphion and Orpheus, two poets of the first ages, one of them, to wit Amphion, built up cities and reared walls with the stones that came in heaps to the sound of his harp—figuring thereby the mollifying of hard and stony hearts by his sweet and eloquent persuasion. And Orpheus assembled the wild beasts . . . implying thereby how by his discrete and wholesome lessons uttered in harmony and with melodious instruments, he brought the rude and savage people to a more civil and orderly life—nothing it seemeth more prevailing or fit to redress and edify the civil and sturdy courage of man than it.

Note that poetry, like oratory, is understood as a source of power. The poet employs "sweet and eloquent persuasion," but it is emphatically persuasion, and its object is to "redress and edify" mankind. The political function of poetry is traced to the beginning of human history and is symbolized in legends like those of Amphion and Orpheus which depict its power to lead "the rude and savage people to a more civil and orderly life." To emphasize the point by contrast, medieval mysticism had stressed passivity, introspection, and illumination. It regarded languages as a vehicle of transcendence—as a means of moving *away* from the natural world to contemplation of the divine, as Dante moves from the human anguish of the *Inferno* to the vision of God in the closing cantos of the *Paradiso*. Conversely, Renaissance humanism stresses life in the world and regards language as a means of influencing social conditions. Petrarch's unfinished epic, *Africa*, is an effort to revive the ancient sense of wordly destiny for fourteenth-century Italy, and Spenser's *Faerie Queene* makes the same effort for the court of Queen Elizabeth. Both are poems of action intended to influence the actions of their readers. As Spenser explained in a letter to Sir Walter Raleigh, the "general end" of *The Faerie Queene* is the fashioning of a perfect gentleman, and he has used the epic form because poetry is a better stimulus to action than philosophy: "so much more profitable is doctrine by example than by rule."

Hercules leads men in chains; the poet leads them with "sweet lessons uttered in harmony"—with the honey on the rim of the medicine cup, the sweet coating on the bitter pill, or, to quote Sidney's *Apology for Poetry*, "a medicine of cherries." As Sidney further explains, "Moving is of a higher degree than teaching . . . for as Aristotle sayeth, it is not *gnosis* but *praxis* must be the fruit."

What the humanists symbolize by their near identifica-   III
tion of the orator and the poet is an ideal harmony between power and beauty. It is an attractive ideal that retained its force throughout the Renaissance. Yet despite Petrarch's public concerns, he was happier in his retreat at Vaucluse than at centers of power like Avignon or Milan. He preferred the *vita otiosa*—the life of study and meditation—to political life, and the tension between the elements that he sought to bring into harmony is clear in his imaginary debate with St. Augustine in the *Secretum*. The same tension is evident in the discussion in Sir Thomas More's *Utopia* of whether or not one should become a councillor of kings. Raphael Hythloday, More's hero, scornfully rejects the opportu-

nity. More, of course, took it, and with just the un-happy results that Raphael had foreseen. Again, if Edmund Spenser celebrates Gloriana's court in *The Faerie Queene*, he bitterly satirizes it in poems like "Mother Hubbard's Tale" and "Colin Clout's Come Home."

Dulce bellum inexpertis—the ideal, it would seem, is sweet until tested. The case of John Milton, the last and perhaps greatest in the proud line of Christian human-ists, illustrates both the ideal and the reason for its inadequacy.

During Milton's youth the gap between power and beauty, between the political concerns of the orator and the human concerns of the poet, was already obvious to those in England with eyes to see. The magic of Eliza-beth's reign—assuming it ever existed outside of a few works of literature—had died with her, and between 1600 and 1640 Englishmen became progressively more disen-chanted with their political system and their state reli-gion. If *The Faerie Queene*—a secular epic—speaks for the idealism of the sixteenth century, the seventeenth-century sense of alienation expresses itself most clearly in two quite different forms of literature—in plays like *Volpone*, *Sejanus*, *The Duchess of Malfi*, and *The Revenger's Tragedy* which reveal the corruption of power; and in the lyric poetry of writers like Donne, Herbert, and Crashaw, which turns away from the outer world of society to the inner world of the self.

For all this, the most important public statement by the young Milton is an impassioned manifesto of humanism that at times seems closer to Pico della Mirandola's *Oration on the Dignity of Man* written in the fifteenth century than to the age that produced *The Advancement of Learning* and *The Leviathan*. Milton's *Seventh Prolusion* was composed for delivery before his fellow students at Cambridge in 1632. Trinity College is not exactly the Capitoline Hill, and we imagine Milton in an academic gown rather than the robe of King Robert of Naples, but again we have an emblem in which the poet appears as an orator. Milton's subject is learning, particularly humanistic learning. The Middle Ages, he says, were condemned to barbarism because of their ignorance; whereas knowledge of the great works of philosophy, history, literature, and science is a solace to the individual, an adornment of social relations, and the best foundation for political power. The relationship between learning and power is made explicit in the following passage:

. . . there have been only two men who have had possession of the whole circle of earth as heaven's gift: Alexander the Great and Augustus Caesar, both of them students of philosophy. Indeed, it is as if they had been divinely provided for humanity as an example of the kind of man to whom the helm and reigns of affairs are to be entrusted.

A decade later Milton was not only advocating reform, he was living it as a propagandist for the Puritan revolution. In *The Reason of Church Government*, he pauses in his diatribe against the religious establishment to comment on the duties of the poet. The first duty he mentions is political. It is to "inbreed and cherish in a great people the seeds of virtue and public civility"; and he assumes at this stage in his career that if he writes an epic it will be a nationalist epic based on "our ancient stories" and celebrating some "king or knight before the conquest"—that is, King Arthur or one of his knights. Clearly, he feels no conflict at this moment between the offices of the orator and the poet. Three years later, in 1644, the polemicist appears in the role of deliberative orator. Milton's *Areopagitica* is organized as a formal oration to Parliament, which Milton honors by comparing it to the ancient Athenian tribunal, the Areopagus. The irony of the fact that the oration was delivered only in Milton's imagination and that its proposals were not so much rejected as totally ignored needs no comment. In spite of this fact, there is no indication that Milton sensed a conflict between his two roles. We know that he spent most of the 1630s in retirement at his father's estate at Horton in order to prepare himself for a career as a poet. Yet the most famous passage in *Areopagitica* is a rejection of the contemplative in favor of the active life:

> I cannot praise a fugitive and cloistered virtue, unexercised and unbreathed, that never sallies out and sees her adversary, but slinks out of the race where the immortal garland is to be run for, not without dust and heat.

Significantly, the passage continues with yet another affirmation of the public role of the poet. Milton's example is Edmund Spenser—

. . . our sage and serious poet Spenser, (whom I dare be known to think a better teacher than Scotus or Aquinas,) describing true temperance under the person of Guion, brings him in with his palmer through the cave of Mammon, and the bower of earthly bliss, that he might see and know, and yet abstain.

As Spenser put it, "of so much more profit is doctrine by example than by rule."

Of course this is commonplace humanist doctrine, even to the contrast between the scholastic theorizing of Dun Scotus and Thomas Aquinas and the persuasive eloquence of *The Faerie Queene*. What is unique is the intensity of Milton's commitment. Earlier humanists had often qualified their reforming zeal with irony, as though they knew in their hearts that their efforts would be ineffectual—that power rests on force; that the orator is more likely to be a politician than a statesman; and that, in the real world, the poet is usually faced with the alternative of flattering a Nero or retiring to the lonely Parnassus of his own psyche—or to a Vaucluse or a Horton. But Milton is passionately sincere. He is the reformer turned revolutionary. Caught up in a national effort to transform society, he is mesmerized by his vision of the future:

Methinks I see in my mind a noble and puissant nation rousing herself like a strong man after sleep, and shaking her invincible locks; methinks I see her as an eagle mewing her mighty youth, and kindling her undazzled eyes at the full midday beam; purging and unscaling her long-abused sight at the fountain itself of heavenly radiance.

This is, I think, the high point of Milton's humanism. It is a synthesis of powerful emotion and magnificent eloquence. The form is a prose oration but the eloquence is in all respects poetic. For a moment (though only in Milton's imagination) the robe of King Robert perfectly sets off the laurels of the poet.

But the mood of exaltation was temporary. Milton was destined to give his sight and a good part of his life to a cause that began as an effort to create a new society, degenerated into a military dictatorship, and ended as a butt of ridicule among its triumphant enemies. *Paradise Lost* is not the national epic that Milton once considered but a religious epic. It is still humanistic in its didacticism—its ambition to justify the ways of God to men—but in it the poet and the orator have become separated. The poet is a blind prophet who turns away from the visible world. Bidding farewell to "the Book of Universal Nature," he cries out to the Spirit:

So much the rather thou celestial light
Shine inward, and the mind through all her powers
Irradiate, there plant eyes, all mist from thence
Purge and disperse, that I may see and tell
Of things invisible to mortal sight.

The orator, meanwhile, is objectified as a character in the poem's action. No passage is a more explicit evocation of the Renaissance ideal of eloquence than the following description of an orator gathering himself for a great public statement:

As when of old some Orator renowned
In Athens or free Rome, where Eloquence
Flourished, since mute, to some great cause addressed,
Stood in himself collected, while each part,
Motion, each act won audience ere the tongue,
Sometimes in height began, as no delay
Or Preface brooking through his Zeal of Right;
So standing, moving, or to height upgrown,
The Tempter all impassioned thus began.

Of course, the passage is bitterly ironic. It is Satan who is preparing to speak. His audience is Eve and his eloquence will bring about the Fall of Man.

The harsh lessons of the Commonwealth years become overt in Milton's *Paradise Regained*, which was written long after the struggle to transform England into the New Jerusalem had been abandoned. In *Paradise Regained* Satan offers Christ the opportunity to do exactly what earlier humanists had dreamed of doing—he offers Christ the political power to translate his ideals into social reform:

With what ease [Satan remarks]
Indued with Regal Virtues as thou art,
Appearing, and beginning noble deeds,
Mightst thou expell [Tiberius] from his Throne
Now made a sty, and in his place ascending
A victor people free from servile yoke.

There is no irony in Christ's reply. It is unambiguous, and, from the humanist point of view, profoundly disillusioned:

What wise and valiant man would seek to free
These thus degenerate, by themselves enslaved,
Or could of inward slaves make outward free.

Whether you approve of these words or not, they constitute a decisive rejection not only of Satan's temptation but of the idea of social reform itself. They thus strike at the heart of the Renaissance belief that the orator and the poet have complementary roles. If society cannot be reformed, then eloquence is useless or worse. It may not be "the first gift of God" as Thomas Wilson believed, but an instrument of tyranny.

As for poetry, there is a movement in *Paradise Regained* toward a new concept of what poetic eloquence should be. The great public abstractions—Duty, Liberty, Justice, the Commonwealth—begin to sound hollow. Milton's Christ seeks a more intimate communication. This is reflected in the fact that the model for the poem was evidently *The Book of Job* rather than the classical epics that lie behind *Paradise Lost*. The dream of the puissant nation stirring itself from slumber is over. In *Paradise Regained*, Rome and Athens, symbolizing human glory and human culture, are mirages seen by Christ from a great distance through what Milton calls "an airy microscope." The setting of *Paradise Regained* is not Eden but the desert. The magnificent effort to create a Christian epic has been succeeded, as Professor Louis Martz has taught us, by something approximating religious meditation.

What I want to stress in this account of Milton's rejection of humanism is that it was forced on him by history. As a young man, Milton eagerly embraced the humanist program of social reform. In the 1640s he lived its success; and in his later years he lived its failure. His response to this failure was a rejection of the idea of the orator-poet based on disillusionment with the possibility of meaningful reform. "So shall the world go on," says Michael summarizing human history to Adam, "to good malignant, to bad men benign."

Milton's solution is a progressively more intense emphasis on the relation of poetry to the inner life of the individual rather than to the life of society. In a famous passage at the end of *Paradise Lost* the angel Michael summarizes the lesson that Adam has learned from his experiences. In its closing lines the passage also suggests what Milton has learned:

This having learned, thou has attained the sum
Of wisdom; hope no higher, though all the Stars
Thou knewest by name, all Nature's works . . .
                        . . . only add
Deeds to thy knowledge answerable, add Faith
Add Virtue, Patience, Temperance, add Love,
By name to come called Charity, the soul
Of all the rest: then wilt thou not be loath
To leave this Paradise, but shalt possess
A Paradise within thee, happier far.

"A Paradise within thee, happier far." This, we assume, is what Petrarch really sought on the lonely slopes

of Parnassus when he described the "inner force divinely
infused in the poet's spirit." The notion that the quest
would advance the glory of the state was an illusion; the
robe of King Robert was ultimately an impediment
rather than an asset.

IV   During the period that I am discussing, the lesson was
existential, if you will permit an overused term. What I
mean is that it was felt but not adequately conceptual-
ized. It could be put in conventional religious terms, but
the vocabulary of Renaissance theology creates as many
problems for anyone who wants to talk about art as the
vocabulary of Renaissance rhetoric. What was needed to
define the function of the artist—and the inner force to
which the artist appeals in other men—was a new vocabulary based on a new concept of the way that art is
related to other human activities.

   I do not wish to become involved in the technicalities
of philosophy, but I do think that the problem encoun-
tered by the humanists was eventually solved. The solution was given toward the end of the eighteenth century
as a corollary of what has been called "the Copernican
Revolution" in philosophy initiated by Kant and his
followers, and it is a solution that remains important in
aesthetic thought today. In terms of my present subject,
its most important feature is its sharp distinction between purposive and nonpurposive activity—between
praxis and *gnosis*—and its assignment of art to the latter

category. Purposive activity is directed to something beyond itself—in the social sphere, to those same public ideas of Duty, Liberty, Justice, and the Republic that so fascinated Milton during the Commonwealth years. Conversely, nonpurposive activity is its own justification. It is inner—not outer—directed. You do not, for example, write a poem to persuade the reader to be virtuous or to strengthen (or to weaken) the state, but to express and communicate experience. And by the same token, reading a poem is not an exercise in moral rearmament or a political indoctrination session, but an enlargement and enrichment of the inner life of the reader.

If this is a valid way of looking at art, and I think it is, it helps us understand better than Milton the source of the recurrent tension during the Renaissance between the claims of social reform and the claims of the "inner force divinely infused in the poet's spirit." The orator and the poet are not cousins—they are not even of the same race. The orator is purposive, and the test of eloquence is action. The role of the poet is not to fashion a higher eloquence, a more persuasive stimulus to action, but to create a medium in language that permits his own inwardness to touch and perhaps illumine the inwardness of others. In contrast to Sidney's claim that the purpose of art is "not *gnosis* but *praxis*" there is Schiller's assertion in his *Letters on the Aesthetic Education of Man*, "If, after [aesthetic] enjoyment . . . we find ourselves impelled to a particular mode of feeling or

action, and unfit for other modes, this serves as infalli-
ble proof that we have not experienced any pure aesthetic effect."

Here, I think, is the view of art toward which Milton
was driven by the frustration of his efforts to combine
the roles assigned him by the humanist theory of art,
but which he could formulate only in the religious image of the "Paradise within thee happier far."

V   Humanism began with the ideal of an order in which
beauty is sustained by power and power fulfilled by
beauty. The ideal retained its fascination throughout the
Renaissance. Men spoke and behaved and organized
their curricula as though the ideal were valid or could be
if only enough orations were delivered and enough
grammar schools founded and enough art works
"cherishing and inbreeding the seeds of virtue and public civility" were written.

Milton was not the last European to be swayed by
this ideal, but his life illustrates its inadequacy with
particular vividness. In view of the programs for social
reform that seem endemic to our own age—and of the
reiterated demands that the modern artist and humanist
place their talents in the service of these programs—the
failure of the Renaissance ideal provides a lesson well
worth remembering. When we are told, as we are being
told today, that the highest value of art is what is called
its "redeeming social function," we will do well to pon-

der the adage that so intrigued Erasmus: *Dulce bellum inexpertis*. You might translate that as "War is sweet to the undrafted." Out of respectful memory of Milton's Eve, I offer another, more homely maxim: "When you sup with the devil, you need a long spoon."

CHAPTER *4*

But how can we speak of mere play, when we know that it is precisely play and play alone, which of all man's states and conditions, is the one which makes him whole and unfolds both sides of his nature at once?

Schiller, *Letters on the Aesthetic
Education of Man*

As the schools appear to fail to teach many children such basic skills as reading and mathematics, the production-line mentality has surfaced as another alternative. Known as performance contracting, such measures have been sponsored by the producers of educational teaching materials and aids. They promise special rewards for successful pupils and teachers—and for the latter, special penalties, too, for failure to produce.

Fred Hechinger, *New York Times*,
February 14, 1971

SUMMERHILL—AND AFTER

A decade of bitter controversy has effectively dispelled any notion that we in the United States possess a consensus in our educational philosophy. We spend approximately $27 billion a year on higher education, we send a larger percentage of high school graduates to college than any other country in the world, and yet instead of taking pride in our achievement, we are driven to the edge of despair by its shortcomings. The national debate on education is typified in President Nixon's speech of March 19, 1970, on reform in higher education. The preamble to the President's text is a litany of complaints, whose every paragraph begins with the phrase "something is basically wrong." The climactic paragraph summarizes these complaints: "Something is wrong with higher education itself when curricula are often irrelevant, structure is often outmoded, when there is an imbalance between teaching and research and too often an indifference to innovation."

Irrelevant, outmoded, unbalanced, indifferent. Clearly, the theory of education—the explanations we offer for what we are doing—has become divorced from the practice of education—what actually occurs in the classroom.

87

There is nothing new or surprising in the separation of theory and practice. It happened in Roman society at the beginning of the Middle Ages. It happened within the Catholic Church at the end of the Middle Ages. It happened in politics in England in 1640 and again in France in 1790. And it is threatening to happen today in American political life.

In any social system, theory and practice tend to coincide at the beginning. As time passes, theory tends to remain static while practice grows and changes in order to adapt to changing conditions. We stand in a river and we never stand in the same water twice. Eventually the tension between the theory and the system it purports to explain becomes acute. When this point is reached three things happen.

First, a reaction sets in. A hue and cry is set up to get back to "the good old days," that is, to force the system back into conformity to the theory. Consider, for example, debate between the liberal and the strict constructionists of the Constitution. Second, new theories, implying entirely new systems, are proposed. Third, modifications of traditional theory that attempt to rationalize existing practice are offered.

If the second approach is radical and a natural consequence of the persistence in society of creative (if not always very helpful) thought, the third is a by-product of the vested interests of those who are in the system, the bureaucrats.

Until recently, the nearest thing to a core theory for American education was what was called "liberal education." The basic concepts of liberal education date back to the fifteenth century. They shaped the curriculum of the English schools and were brought to this country by English colonists. During the nineteenth century they were adopted by American private schools and the Ivy League colleges and universities. They were imitated outside of New England, and their continued vitality is indicated by the widespread popularity up to ten years ago of great books courses, classics in translation, and general education.

So much misinformation has circulated about the liberal arts curriculum that one point needs to be stressed heavily. The Renaissance humanists who invented it were almost obsessively practical. They attacked medieval culture for being impractical, and they wanted to reform society. Their educational system was to be the chief instrument for accomplishing this reform. If the object of medieval education was mastery of scripture, the object of the Renaissance humanists was a thorough understanding of the ways of the world aimed at elevating human life to the level of nobility. They required mastery of Greek and Latin because in the fifteenth and sixteenth centuries most of the knowledge they considered essential—especially knowledge of eloquence—was found in the classics. They wrote in Latin because Latin was an international language. Unlike the enlightened intelligentsia of the twentieth century, Renaissance humanists—whether Poles, Germans, Italians, or Englishmen—could converse freely through the medium of Latin.

The humanists stressed rhetoric because it trained people to speak effectively. Their goal was to create an intellectual elite from which the state would draw its magistrates, its governors, its jurists, its parliamentarians, and its educators. Precisely because they were training an elite, the humanists emphasized the liberal arts. They included literature at every level of the curriculum not because it was enjoyable but because it could be used to teach ethical values (you learn courage from Achilles) and rhetorical skills (even Ovid's *Art of Love* can teach you something useful about personification, metaphor, and balanced constructions).

Today, arguments for general as against specialized education, for spreading course work over a series of electives before entering a major, for making the humanities the center of the curriculum, and for the morally elevating effect of a liberal arts program all testify to the vitality of humanist thought. It can even be argued that the demands of the New Left that education be used for political indoctrination simply repeat for the twentieth century the equally fervent political demands of Renaissance educators.

By the nineteenth century, humanist theory, although unchallenged as theory, was no longer adequate to explain educational practice. At the traditional schools, efforts were made to modernize the curriculum by substituting modern languages and literature for Greek and Latin. But traditional schools aside, a whole new educational system was being called into existence

SUMMERHILL—AND AFTER 91

by the industrial revolution. The appetite of the emerging industrial economy for machinists, engineers, chemists, metallurgists, architects, industrial designers, and economists was limitless, and inevitably schools appeared to train them. In the United States the demand shaped the emergent land-grant colleges created by the Morrill Act of 1862 and led to such institutions as MIT, Cal Tech, VPI, and Case Institute. Although the trend at such institutions since World War II has been away from narrowly vocational training, President Nixon's March 1970 speech makes it clear that the government prescription for the 1970s will involve more, not less vocationalism:

I propose [the President says] to create a career education program funded at $100 million in fiscal 1972 to assist states and institutions in meeting the additional costs of starting new programs to teach critically-needed skills in community colleges and technical institutions.

And later:

Too many people have fallen prey to the myth that a four-year, liberal-arts diploma is essential to a full and rewarding life; whereas, in fact, other forms of postsecondary education—such as a two-year community college or technical training course—are far better suited to the interests of many young people.

Whether too many people have fallen prey to the myth of the liberal arts may be debated with some acrimony by those who believe they are fighting for the survival of those same liberal arts. But that problem aside, it is clear enough how the wind blows in Washington. It blows vocational.

The point is that vocational education is quite different from liberal education. As I have already pointed out, proponents of the liberal arts from the Renaissance to the 1950s consistently opposed vocational education as being narrow, overspecialized, and unsuited to the constantly changing conditions of life outside the classroom. Vocational education is supported by a single argument which has the virtue of simplicity if not of sophistication. It trains people for jobs. Although it is usually explained as being socially useful, it has no innate ideological commitment. The same computer technology that deposited Michael Collins on the moon will, in the fullness of time, deposit a Russian cosmonaut there. The same metallurgy that produced armor plate for the Defense Department produced armor-piercing shells for Hitler's *Wehrmacht*. And the same fertilizer that grows corn in Ohio and pollutes Lake Erie grows wheat in the Crimea and pollutes the Black Sea.

Vocational education *per se* is neutral. The failures resulting from Lysenko's attempt to impose Communism on genetics—or of Hitler's banishment of "Jewish physics" from his Aryan laboratories—show that this condition is not an accident but a fundamental imperative. If you violate the neutrality of vocational education—if you insist on "Aryan" physics or "Marxist" genetics—you subvert its object. And here, precisely, is the weakness of vocational education. It trains servants of a system—any system—not responsible citizens. If technology causes irreversible ecological damage, too bad. If it leads to an arms race with nuclear war as a possible outcome, too bad. The contention of the New Left that American education is the youth corps of the military-industrial complex is valid insofar as American education is vocational. But it applies equally to vocational education in Cuba or the People's Republic of China or Russia or South Africa.

If my argument so far has been general, it is correct, I believe, in its larger outlines. We have two well-defined systems of education in the United States. (I emphasize the word *systems*, for I am not now considering experiments, no matter how important.) The first is traditional. It is supported by a well-developed philosophy, it is social and ethical in its goals, and it involves heavy emphasis on the humanities. It is currently being attacked for irrelevance and elitism. The second has only a primitive rationale and was created more or less ad hoc by the industrial revolution. It is vocational, correlated to the needs of industry, and has no necessary humanistic content. It has always been criticized for its narrowness, and it is now being attacked for producing lackeys to a corrupt system. Liberal education is socially oriented, while vocational education is information- and skill-oriented. The goal of the first is nobility; of the second, jobs.

II

There is a third force in contemporary education. It is a powerful force but it is difficult to define. Because I wish to call attention to its historical roots, I will call it aesthetic education. A more familiar—but more imprecise—label is progressive education.

The theory underlying aesthetic education was formulated at a specific moment in history, the Romantic period. In the preceding chapter, I noted the recurrent tension in humanism that often produced tragic conflicts in the lives of individual humanists. My prime example was John Milton. I suggested that Renaissance humanists were compelled to suffer this tension because nothing in their frame of reference allowed them to identify its source. The Kantian revolution at the end of the eighteenth century changed all that. For Kant and his followers, imagination, not reason (or even emotion), is the primary human faculty. The life of the imagination is aesthetic experience. This life is natural, instinctive, and profoundly human. If the need for imaginative experience is ignored, individuals—eventually whole societies—suffer.

The primary characteristic of aesthetic experience is that it is its own end. It is characterized, to use Kant's phrase, by purposiveness without purpose. It benefits the individual by enriching his inner life, but it is neither ideologically committed nor economically useful. It does not lead to a specific moral orientation or a specific political philosophy, nor does it equip individuals with vocational skills. Indeed, the opposite is true. A

culture or an educational system that demands a particular moral or political outlook or a specific set of skills
does so at the expense of imagination. The imaginative
function must be recognized and cultivated. If this function is natural, as the Romantics claimed, its repression
will be unnatural and damaging. Often it will be
achieved only by brute force. Recall Heinrich Heine's
remark that the chief difference between regular and
irregular verbs is that you get whipped more for the
irregulars.

So far as I know, the first effort to relate Kantian
ideas to the social function of the humanities was
Schiller's *Letters on the Aesthetic Education of Man*,
written around 1795. Schiller wrote in terms of the
informal education that is the natural result of the adult
experience of art. Some forty years earlier a more intuitive and sentimental version of aesthetic education had
been developed by Rousseau in *Émile*. The two authors—Rousseau and Schiller—are almost antithetical in
tone, but they meet on certain fundamentals. The first
is that education should be natural and enjoyable rather
than repressive. The second is that it should be directed
at individual development rather than abstract, socially
approved goals. The third is that it should liberate rather
than confine and intimidate. The fourth is that most
normal human beings have a potential for this type of
education although the potential is usually ignored and
frequently undermined or destroyed by formal education and social conditioning.

It is not true that the Romantic period invented the child, but it *is* true that the modern concept of childhood is essentially Romantic. For the generation following Rousseau and Kant the child embodied all that is human and natural, while adult sensibility appeared to be dulled by stereotypes and conventions. The child in this view is not conditioned. His emotions are spontaneous. In other words, he responds imaginatively, while the adult is cut off from the world by his education and his social experiences. Consider, for example, Wordsworth's sonnet to his daughter Caroline. After eight rather ponderous lines describing his own response to the beauty of the scene before him, Wordsworth turns to the girl:

Dear Child! Dear Girl! that walkest with me here,
If thou appear untouched by solemn thought,
Thy nature is not therefore less divine:
Thou liest in Abraham's bosom all the year;
And worshipp'st at the Temple's inner shrine,
God being with thee when we know it not.

And in still more famous lines Wordsworth exclaims:

Heaven lies about us in our infancy!
Shades of the prison-house begin to close
    Upon the growing Boy,
But He beholds the light, and whence it flows,
    He sees it in its joy;
The Youth, who daily further from the east

Must travel, still is Nature's Priest,
And by the vision splendid
Is on his way attended;
At length the Man perceives it die away,
And fade into the light of common day.

Does it have to die away? This is the question which the Romantic movement posed for education. A child is born natural and learns to be unnatural. Is the process inevitable? In *Émile* Rousseau advised teachers, "The first thing is to study your pupils more, for it is very certain that you do not know them." Since Rousseau, almost all attempts to put Romantic theory into practice have grown out of theories about child psychology. Pestalozzi, Herbart, Mayo, Montessori, and Dewey were all theorists of elementary education. In fact, it is only in the last few decades that extensive efforts have been made to apply Romantic principles to later stages of education.

One of the most interesting modern experiments in aesthetic education is the school Summerhill founded in England some forty years ago by A. S. Neill and described in his book *Summerhill: A Radical Approach to Child Rearing*. The chief quarrel I have with this remarkable book is its title, for if you have been following my argument you will see that there is nothing radical in Neill's approach. It is unique in details, but in outline and purpose it is simply one man's version of a tradition as old as the Romantic period.

In the first place, Summerhill is oriented entirely toward the individual. It is a boarding school with about forty pupils ranging in age from seven to eighteen. Neill attempts to maintain a relaxed and intimate friendship between students and staff. Staff members are taught not to act as authority figures but equals, and in the school councils where policy is decided the youngest first-grader has the same vote as Neill himself.

In the second place, Summerhill has a minimal structure. Students are grouped informally within three categories according to age (a concession to Freud), but any student may attend any class. Division into formal grades is eliminated, as is the assignment of grades for achievement. Students can take courses or not as they like. According to Neill, some are so thoroughly alienated by conventional education that years pass after their arrival at Summerhill before they ask to join a learning group. As a corollary, the school makes no effort to teach a religious or social code or a specified body of knowledge. Neill considers conventional religion antagonistic to natural development. As for moral training, Neill writes, *"I believe that it is moral instruction that makes the child bad. I find that when I smash the moral instruction a bad boy has received, he becomes a good boy."* And as for a body of knowledge or a set of skills—vocational education—the lack of a standard curriculum makes this impossible by definition. Summerhill makes no attempt to prepare students for college entrance examinations or even for the job market. Neill is almost boastful of the students who drifted after they left Summerhill and seems openly proud of the number of graduates who elected *not* to enter universities. His educational goal is purely and simply the inner well-being of the individual:

The function of the child is to live his own life—not the life that his anxious parents think he should lead, nor a life according to the purpose of an educator who thinks he knows what is best. All of this interference and guidance on the part of adults only produces a generation of robots.

"Shades of the prison-house begin to close/Upon the growing Boy." In Neill's arrangements we see the Romantic ideal of freedom and natural behavior. The alienated student, according to this point of view, comes to school in psychological fetters. Not until the fetters are removed can the process of inner development go forward. Education is not an imposing of standards but a removing of barriers. The credo of Summerhill is that when truly free, when truly natural, the student will be eager to work and work hard to achieve his goals. In other words, motivation is natural and lack of it a sickness contracted from family, society, and a perverse educational system.

The Romantics believed that what is natural is also enjoyable, and they celebrated the joy of primary experiences, of childhood, of life lived close to nature, of powerful emotions that break through social conventions. For the same reason Neill insists that happiness is both the condition and end of education. Conventional schooling is imposed by fear—fear of punishment, fear of failure, fear of disapproval. "The absence of fear," writes Neill, "is the finest thing that can happen to a child." Schiller long ago traced the creative activity of the artist and the re-creative activity of the audience to the *Spieltrieb*—the play impulse. Play, as he saw it, is a self-justified and self-fulfilling experience. Neill makes the same point: "Most of the school work that adolescents do is simply a waste of time, of energy, of patience. It robs youth of its right to play and play and play. . . . It puts old heads on young shoulders."

For Neill, play is the most important childhood activity. In fact, Neill criticizes the Montessori method because instead of allowing play for its own sake it attempts to use play to teach standard subjects, an approach also taken by the writers of *Sesame Street*. "I hold," writes Neill, "that the aim of life is to find happiness, which means to find interest. Education should be a preparation for life."

Two further characteristics of Neill's approach deserve mention. First, although Summerhill does not teach any moral system, Neill believes that the result of his training will be moral improvement. In this he again recalls Schiller, who believed that one of the by-products of aesthetic education would be a gradual refinement of the individual. The argument rests on the assumption that most antisocial activity is the result of maladjustment, usually socially induced. Remove the cause and the antisocial activity will disappear in all but the most deeply scarred individuals. There is an element of naïve exaggeration—even of Pelagianism—in Neill's arguments here, but they bear quoting all the same:

No happy man ever disrupted a meeting, or produced a war, or lynched a Negro. No happy woman ever nagged her husband or her children. No happy man ever frightened his employees.

All crimes, all hatreds, all wars can be reduced to unhappiness. This book is an attempt to show . . . how children can be reared so that much unhappiness will never arise.

Second, like the Romantics before him, Neill is radically nominalistic. He distrusts systems just as Romantic poets distrusted the abstract nouns and easy personifications of neo-classic poetry and sought instead a specific expression for each specific experience. Neill provides individual psychotherapy sessions for his students. Other than that, he disclaims any general method of teaching. It is the attitude of the student rather than the method of the teacher or the school that is important:

We do not consider that teaching in itself matters very much. Whether or not a school has or has not a special method for teaching long division is of no significance, for long division is of no importance except to those who want to learn it. And the child who *wants* to learn long division *will* learn it no matter how it is taught.

These words may seem a little bizarre against the current backdrop of demands for improved teaching, teacher evaluation, and fool-proof methodology, but they deserve to be heard.

III   Anyone familiar with American education will be aware of dozens of experiments like Summerhill in this country. The interesting fact about the present situation is that the concept of education represented by Summerhill seems to be spreading from the primary schools to the high schools and colleges. In some few cases this development may be due to a conscious philosophy. For the most part, however, it seems to be the result of empirical research by educational psychologists, and, above all, dissatisfaction on the part of students and teachers with what the schools have to offer. Whatever the source, the demands that are pushing education toward Summerhill include elimination of grades, abolition of course requirements, abandonment of the lecture system in favor of small discussion groups—and abandonment of discussion groups in favor of tutorials and independent study, integration of subjects studied with personal interests, and elimination of regulations governing student life.

These are not isolated or eccentric demands. They are the testimony of an entire generation. I am not sure whether the demands can be met or where they would lead if met, but there is no doubt whatever of their urgency.

If we can now find a pattern in what at first glance IV
seemed chaotic, the pattern is formed by the interaction
of three distinct traditions in contemporary education.
The source of confusion is that no tradition ever appears
in undiluted form, while in debates about the aims of
education the three traditions become hopelessly tan-
gled. Two of the traditions—the liberal and the aesthetic—are deeply sympathetic to the humanities,
though for different reasons. The third, the vocational,
is indifferent if not hostile to them.

So much for the present. We are obviously in the
midst of rapid changes in our educational system. Is it
possible to predict the direction that the changes will
take in the near future? I stress "near future" since for
reasons that I will discuss in the next chapter, I feel that
things may change very radically in the more distant
future.

I think so, for I think that during the next few years
the shape of American education will be determined
largely by two factors, both of them political.

The first is sufficiently clear from President Nixon's
speech on education. You will recall that the President
places special emphasis on vocational education. The
reason is simple and hard to dismiss. Poverty is one of
our chief national problems, and the official explanation
for much of that poverty is lack of job skills. Whether
the explanation is valid is another matter. There are
reasons for believing that unemployment is a corollary

of advanced technological culture rather than of inadequate job skills, but for now we can move to the second factor.

The second factor, which may eventually be as influential as the desire to prepare people for jobs, is the public's demand for ways to measure the effectiveness of public education. If vocational education reflects the imperative of industrial society to correlate all human activity to production, the urge to measure reflects the myth of industrial society that what cannot be quantified does not exist.

The operative words here are "productivity" and "accountability." Both of them are imports from business. President Nixon sounded the keynote for the administration in a speech on March 3, 1970, announcing that educators have "too long avoided thinking of the productivity of the schools." This initiative was duly expanded in a speech on March 30 of that year by James Allen, Jr., then U.S. Commissioner of Education, announcing that "the people have a right to be assured that the increasingly large investments in public education . . . will produce results." To make results certain Allen endorsed the idea of an "independent accomplishment audit" and "performance contracts" whereby the school would farm out its programs to private firms in return for guaranteed results.

A hint of what was anticipated is furnished by a news release shortly after Allen's speech from the Regional Education Laboratory of Durham, North Carolina, which, incidentally, was supported in 1970 by $820,000 from the Office of Education. The news release begins:

Twelve faculty members at John Tyler Community College in Chester, Virginia, have signed "performance agreements" that their teaching will produce specific, measurable results in their students.

In essence each of the teachers agreed that he would be able to provide evidence when his class ended that his students could master the objectives of his course.

The 12 teachers are members of the humanities department. Only those faculty members who participate in the program will be eligible for "merit" pay increases next year.

John E. Rouche, Director of the Laboratory's Junior College division, explains the philosophy behind accountability:

No longer can it be assumed that learning occurs because a teacher is present in the classroom. If no measurable evidence of learning can be exhibited, we must infer that no teaching occurred.

It is not enough to say, "We have provided the opportunity—take it or leave it." We must say that we will be accountable for making teaching relevant to demonstrated student learning.

There are some fifteen regional laboratories around the country.

Private enterprise is also entering the scene. Kenneth Clark, for example, a distinguished New York psychologist, organized an educational consulting firm in 1970 and signed a contract with the District of Columbia school system on April 3 of that year to provide "accountability." When someone asked if the approach would create difficulties, the head of the District School Board replied with robust jocularity, "We certainly will be throwing a monkey wrench into a smooth and easy system where teachers and students show up each day and no one knows what happens."*

The push toward accountability is government-supported and has a sure-fire appeal to the layman who has always been inclined to suspect that "no one knows what happens" in education. In 1970 the government awarded some $7 million in contracts to six companies for eighteen separate programs. Its effects are multiplied by educational technology. That is, complementing the demand for standardized tests to measure results, we have a rapidly growing array of gadgetry that disseminates canned information and determines how much of this information has been memorized by students. The gadgets vary from simple devices that can be used in conjunction with programmed texts, to overhead projectors and sound-and-image-linked filmstrip projectors, to

*The Clark program became the subject of bitter controversy after its enactment and is now all but a dead issue. "Accountability" remains popular with federal and state officials and with school boards, although teachers' unions have pointed to its obvious flaws. "Performance contracts" are in disrepute. They have proven expensive and no more efficient (sometimes less efficient) than what the schools themselves are doing. Cf. the article "Poor Performance" in *Newsweek*, Feb. 14, 1972, p. 97.

video-tape systems with generation as well as replication capability, to computer-display systems that are alleged to dupe young users into believing that they are in contact with human intelligence.

All of this equipment from the simplest to the most Rube Goldbergian has two characteristics. It is expensive and its material is dull. It is produced by corporations like Xerox and IBM and Encyclopedia Britannica, and it involves large investments—obviously, in the hope of large payoffs. School systems are often sold the equipment on the grounds that it saves money by reducing staff needs. What really happens is that costs remain the same or rise, but once the investment has been made the commitment to gadgetry is irreversible. Control of the curriculum begins to pass from the teacher to the accounting office on the one hand and the company research team on the other. The teacher's function is to tend the machine, frighten students into silence during the video-tape program, and ask a few questions during the weekly discussion period.

As for dullness, the information regurgitated by the gadgets is standardized and predigested. As long as human beings are teaching there is an outside chance for the unexpected. But technology excels in repeating the expected. Teaching machines cannot teach anything but their own programs. A filmed lecture, even a lecture by Sir Kenneth Clark, is frozen forever, whereas the most hidebound pedant will make a few changes each time he shuffled through his pile of tattered and yellowed notes.

Machines do not offer education, they offer information. At the end of a preprogramed, audiovisual, computer-monitored course the last thing you do is ask the student whether he is more open, more creative, more responsive across a wider spectrum. What you ask him is how much information he has memorized. This is another way of saying that you evaluate him in terms of the degree to which he has come to resemble a machine.

A. S. Neill and Charles Silberman warn that our present school system is operated through the regular use of intimidation and shame and gradually dehumanizes its victims, one symptom of this process being that it turns so many of them permanently against learning. If so, what will be the effect of the alliance between accountability and technology? I suspect that the last shreds of humanity, the last vestiges of willingness on the part of the teacher to consider the individual and let the system go hang will be threatened. Whatever the teacher might want to do, he will no longer be a free agent. He will have joined the victims. His intellectual freedom will be diminished by the fact that his future depends on how well his pupils satisfy the test-makers and the computers. And his emotional freedom will be diminished by fear—fear for his livelihood, for his prospects for advancement, for his self-respect. Meanwhile, if accountability threatens the aesthetic element in contemporary education it also implies the diversion of liberal education from its traditional ethical concerns to the accumulation of the facts, dates, and one hundred standard opinions that are the regular fare of the machine-graded examination.

I have not looked very far into the future, but I believe V
that the short-term signs point toward vocationalism, accountability, and the rise of gadgetry in public education. In the private sector there will be resistance from both aesthetic and liberal educators, but the need for sufficient matching of programs to permit easy two-way migration between public and private systems will have some effect. The point is that if the concept of education represented by Summerhill is even partially valid, we are moving in the wrong direction. We are moving in the wrong direction in terms of our present responsibilities and we are moving in the wrong direction in terms of our responsibilities to the future.

CHAPTER 5

Nothing could be more misleading to our children than our present affluent society. They will inherit a totally different world, a world in which the standards, politics, and economics of the past are dead. As the most influential nation in the world today, and its largest consumer, the United States cannot stand isolated. We are today involved in events leading to famine and ecocatastrophe; tomorrow we may be destroyed by them.

Paul Ehrlich, *The Population Bomb*

Far from being an expression of an irrational flight from the machine, the decision to kill the SST was, we believe, testimony to the new technological sophistication which refuses to believe that man is subordinate to technology.

New York Times editorial, March 28, 1971

AN OLD AGE IS OUT:
INDUSTRIAL SOCIETY AND
THE FUTURE OF HUMANISM

You can make a hobby today of collecting doomsday books. Barbara Ward, Rachel Carson, George Wald, Charles Silberman, Paul Ehrlich, Zbigniew Brzezinski (unpronounceable oracle), Jacques Cousteau, Jay W. Forrester, Harold York, Charles Reich, Eldridge Cleaver, and Alvin Toffler are names that spring immediately to mind, but the list is not even remotely complete and it grows apace. Within the last year Donella and Dennis Meadows, two MIT scientists supported by The Club of Rome, have dropped what may be a crystal in the supersaturated solution of doomsday thinking through their book *The Limits to Growth*.

The Limits to Growth is written in computer jargon, and its assumptions have been dismissed as simplistic by almost everybody who is anybody. Probably so. But surely the real point is that the Meadows have done little more than say with graphs what other experts, including some of their critics, have been saying in plain English for the last ten years—a message reiterated by several highly respected international authorities at the Stockholm environmental conference of June 1972.

The sense of crisis that underlies *The Limits to Growth* and the communiqués of the Stockholm conference began to dominate European and American intellectual life after World War I. Oswald Spengler's *Decline of the West* and T. S. Eliot's *Wasteland* have a common theme: we are coming to the end of an era. Perhaps not only an era but a whole cycle of civilization. Since World War II what was once regarded as a malaise of the intellectuals has spread to all areas of society. Most people who read the newspapers would, I assume, agree with the following comment by C. P. Snow in the September 7, 1970 issue of the *Times Literary Supplement*:

We are walking with complacency into a situation more ominous than any in recent history: different from previous dangers but quite possibly worse than any the human race has known. This is the situation in which those whose education we are now discussing will be living in early middle age.

The reasons for Lord Snow's anxiety are familiar, but at the risk of stating the obvious, I will summarize them under three heads. First, we have created a kind of warfare so savage that no one is certain whether, in the event of a major conflict, there will be survivors, much less victors. If Harold York is correct in his book *Race to Oblivion*, our security against nuclear war is currently diminishing rather than increasing. Even if his argument is overstated (and the SALT agreements of 1972 give some reason to hope that they are), we appear to be powerless to effectively limit the spread of atomic weapons to nonnuclear powers.

Second, we know that human population is expanding catastrophically. Within this century, world population may double from 3.5 billion to 7 billion. According to population experts like Paul Ehrlich and Professor Kingsley Davis of the Berkeley, California, Urban Planning Authority, within seventy years—the life-span of a child born today—world population may reach 15 billion. Most of these future citizens will live in the poorest nations, and no one is certain they can be supported at all. Quite aside from humanitarian concern for their welfare, the existence of vast numbers of human beings living at or below the subsistence level can only increase international tension and consequently the chance of war.

Third, we know that every effort we make to improve the living conditions of the world population, whether in New York City or Bombay, India, has adverse as well as beneficial effects. In many parts of the world, pollution has already reached a critical stage, and we are now hearing warnings about possible irreversible damage to the biosphere itself—the system that supports planetary life. As Lord Ritchie-Calder wrote in *Foreign Affairs* in January 1970, "There are no frontiers in present-day pollution and destruction of the biosphere. Mankind shares a common habitat. We have mortgaged the old homestead, and nature is liable to foreclose." The graphs in *The Limits to Growth* confirm this opinion. And if things are bad already, they can only be made worse by the rising expectations of the underdeveloped nations. Try to imagine the environmental damage that would accompany any honest effort to export Western standards of living to the three-fourths of world population *now* living in poverty—I am not speaking here of the doubled population of the year 2000. The trauma to the world's atmosphere and water supply created by a three-fold increase in current levels of production could only be terminal given the present state of technology.

Evidently we are reaching the end of the industrial revolution. This is not a particularly original observation but it is worth repeating. I do not mean that the production lines in Detroit are going to shut down tomorrow or that we have seen the last of technological innovation. What I mean is that wherever we look we find that the very success of Western man has brought him to the point of negative returns. His brilliant technology has produced weapons that may destroy him. His humane medicine has eliminated natural controls on population growth. His cornucopian industry has befouled the air and water, destroyed organic patterns of living, and glutted the physical environment with things and the psychological environment with propaganda and ersatz culture.

In its long pioneering journey, industrial society appears finally to be approaching the Pacific Ocean. We have not reached the Pacific Ocean but we can begin to make out the shoreline. I say this not as a lament or a cry of despair but as a fact. Either we confront reality and accommodate ourselves to it or we go the way of the dinosaurs. I will add that I am by no means ready to admit that the situation is hopeless. It is critical. It is, in Lord Snow's words, "quite possibly worse than any [danger] the human race has known." But it is probably not hopeless.

Before offering suggestions about what lies ahead, I want to comment further on what we are leaving behind. I will limit my comments to two aspects of industrial man: his materialism and his discontents.   II

    To appreciate the rationale of industrialism you need to recall that from the time of Plato to the Renaissance, philosophers thought of society as static, hierarchic, and ordered by divinely sanctioned or rationally self-evident laws. Fulfillment for the citizen consisted in performing the duties appropriate to his class. Social mobility was considered dangerous. "Take but degree away," wrote Shakespeare in *Troilus and Cressida*, "and hark what discord follows." The beehive was a traditional symbol for this idea: stable, harmonious, and contented. There is a charming and typical use of the beehive symbol in the first act of Shakespeare's *Henry V*. The Bishop of Canterbury is giving his version of the perfect society:

so work the honey-bees
Creatures that by a rule in nature teach

The act and order of a peopled kingdom.
They have a king and officers of sorts
Where some, like magistrates, correct at home,
Others, like merchants, venture trade abroad;
Others, like soldiers, armed in their stings,
Make boot upon the summer's velvet buds,
Which pillage they with merry march bring home
To the tent-royal of their emperor;
Who, busied with his majesty surveys
The singing masons building roofs of gold.

In contrast to the society of bees, industrial society is dynamic. Oswald Spengler identified this dynamism with the myth of Faust as adapted by Goethe at the beginning of the nineteenth century. According to Spengler, the appetite of modern man is infinite. He never rests in achievement but regards each accomplishment as preparation for the next. He is not cooperative, but competitive; and instead of building beehives he creates highways that permit endless, restless movement, and skyscrapers that menace the heavens. As the angels lead Faust's soul to heaven at the end of Goethe's play, they chant the motto of Faustian Man:

Wer immer strebend sich bemüht
Den können wir erlösen:

The man who ceaselessly strives—
Him we can forgive.

Faustian echoes can be heard everywhere in nineteenth-century thought: in Hegel's dialectic which teaches that man is committed to a quest for ever higher levels of spiritual perfection; in the art and poetry that celebrate a journey—to quote Tennyson—"ever onward, ever upward, down the ringing grooves of change"; and in Darwin's concept of continuous evolution, with the corollary, so evident to Nietzsche and George Bernard Shaw, of an *Übermensch*—a superior being who will eventually replace his evolutionary inferior *homo sapiens.*

Whatever may be said for Hegel or Tennyson or Darwin, the dominant expression of the Faustian impulse in the nineteenth and twentieth centuries has been material. Spiritual perfection is impossible to measure even if you grant that it is desirable. On the other hand, improvements in the Gross National Product and the national standard of living are easy to measure and almost universally applauded. One chicken is an improvement over no chickens. A Datsun is an improvement over a Honda. A ten-room house is an improvement over a five-room house. Two houses are better than one, and three are better. . . .

The Faustian impulse materializes itself in the gospel of progress. It is spread abroad by mass advertising, which first became possible with the increase in mass literacy during the nineteenth century and reassures industrial man that each new possession is a new increment of happiness, a step forward toward an elusive something called success. It becomes incarnate in the unnumbered products of industrial technology, from the barest essentials like mass-produced socks to the most exotic and useless luxuries—aerosol deodorants, aluminum beer cans, electric tooth brushes, Winnebago Motor Homes, the pleasure domes of Las Vegas.

Since the Faustian appetite is infinite, there is no level of affluence that either the individual or society can consider final. Both the individual and society are driven in the name of progress to improve on past achievement. If the Gross National Product is 800 billion, the next budget must produce one trillion. If the wage settlement in Detroit is $7.00 per hour, both union and management know that their survival depends on $10.00 at the next bargaining session. If you purchase a Ford this year, you will feel compelled to move up to a Buick—or a vacation cottage by an artificial lake—next. Indeed, the Faustian impulse reaches beyond the grave since among the many burdens that we place on our children is the imperative to outperform their parents. You are not supposed to repeat your father's career—you are supposed to improve on it.

These attitudes are being questioned today but chiefly in the most affluent nations and there chiefly by the most affluent citizens. By and large the masses still accept the industrial creed for the simple reason that in spite of exploitation, brutality, and periodic depressions it has paid off. Because of its success it has been the chief export of Western society to the rest of the world, and today the recurrent themes of politicians in the underdeveloped as well as the developed nations are capital accumulation, production quotas, economic growth, and improved standards of living—what Stuart Udall once called "the tyranny of the GNP." In fact, Western methods have been so successful that world Communism has had to rest its case largely on the promise that it offers a short-cut to Western affluence. Recall Nikita Khrushchev's famous boast that Russia's standard of living would equal America's by 1980. In a recent book on business organization no less a person than Gherman Gvishiani, the son-in-law of Aleksei Kosygin, observed, "Most important for the victory of our social system is superiority in competition with capitalist productivity of labor." If this comment were not so deadpan, it might be faintly amusing, like the joke that used to circulate in Iron Curtain countries on the difference between capitalism and communism: "Capitalism is the exploitation of one class by another. Under Communism just the opposite occurs."

My point is serious. Today the cult of progress has become both a world philosophy and the closest thing we have to a world religion. This has happened at just the moment when the practical limits of material progress are becoming glaringly obvious.

Now for my second point which is concerned with the discontents of industrial man. I have already suggested that preindustrial societies were by and large stable societies and that their central value was the value of participation in a common enterprise. Recall the society of bees. Conversely, Faust's pact with Mephistopheles states that if he ever exclaims, "Let this moment stay, it is so beautiful"—"*Verweile doch! du bist so schön*"—he will be damned. Tennyson's Ulysses, home from his wanderings, finds the contentments of hearth and home intolerable and sets sail again vowing (as everyone knows) "to strive, to seek, to find, and not to yield," while Browning proclaimed, in an equally familiar line, that "a man's grasp should exceed his reach, or what's a heaven for?" But the true Homer of the industrial revolution is Karl Marx. Here is what Marx says in the *Communist Manifesto*—which is brilliant poetry, whatever else it may or may not be—about the dynamics of industrial society:

The bourgeoisie, wherever it has got the upper hand, has put an end to all feudal, patriarchal idyllic relations. It has piteously torn asunder the motly feudal ties that bound man to his "natural superiors" and has left no other bond between man and man but naked self-interest, than callous "cash payment." It has drowned the most heavenly extasies of religious fervor, of chivalrous enthusiasm, of philistine sentimentalism in the icy waters of egotistical calculation. It has resolved personal worth into exchange value, and in place of numberless indefeasible chartered freedoms, has set up that single unconscionable freedom—Free Trade. . . .

The bourgeoisie cannot exist without constantly revolutionizing the instruments of production, and thereby the relations of production, and with them the whole relations of society. Conservation of the old modes of production was the first condition of all earlier industrial classes. Constant revolutionizing of production, uninterrupted disturbances of all social conditions, everlasting uncertainty and agitation, distinguish the bourgeois epoch from all earlier ones. All fixed, fact-frozen relations, with their train of ancient and venerable prejudices and opinions are swept away, all new-formed ones become antiquated before they can ossify. All that is solid melts in the air, and man is at last compelled to face with sober senses his real conditions of life and his relations with his kind.

If it seemed true in 1848 that society depends on "constant revolutionizing of production" with the corollary of "uninterrupted disturbance of all social conditions," it seems far truer today. The growth of technology is geometric not arithmetic. As Alvin Toffler reminds us in *Future Shock*, the rate of social change induced by technology has consistently accelerated since the early nineteenth century, and it will continue to accelerate in the future.

But the human mind is not a machine to be reprogramed every ten years. This is why Toffler's book, whatever its shortcomings, is an important humanistic document. After adolescence we change only slowly, with resistance, and at considerable psychological cost. Increasingly, therefore, as Faustian man has realized his ideal of constant progress he has found himself an alien in his own world. This is Toffler's thesis. It seems to me to be confirmed by direct observation. That is, I think one can see obvious signs of tension everywhere in American society, in the lives of those we know personally as well as in the headlines. There is no point, however, in arguing whether Toffler's fears are exaggerated. What is clear is that industrial society has always exacted a high price for its benefits and that we can foresee a time in the future when the price may be more than we want to pay. I have already suggested that the material achievement of the industrial revolution has reached the point of negative returns. I now add that the spiritual burden of industrialism—the need to adjust to constant progress and constant change—may also be reaching some kind of a limit. The Faustian dream is threatening to become a nightmare.

III   None of this is very comforting, I realize. My only excuse for mentioning it is that it bears directly on my next theme—the future of humanism. What I have been describing is apparently a material and economic crisis; but equally, if less visibly, it is an inner crisis, a crisis of values as Spengler and T. S. Eliot long ago recognized. To understand this is to confront the inevitability of a major revision of the values traditional to industrial culture. I do not mean that the old values are evil or intentionally destructive. I simply mean that according to the best evidence we now have these values are becoming anachronistic. They are not going to disappear overnight but sooner or later they will be replaced by values more in keeping with our real situation.

It is here that the humanistic point of view begins to be central. One way of describing modern society is to say that it is a society in which things and the economic forces generated by things are allowed to take precedence over human values. This is one of the meanings of Mary Shelley's fable in which the monster created by

Dr. Frankenstein's science threatens to destroy its maker. It is also the meaning of the innumerable adjustments of priorities, political, military, and social, in which—since the beginning of this century—things and impersonal forces have been allowed to take precedence over human interests and people. Moon rockets have been more important than malnutrition; balance sheets have been more important than slums; national prestige has been more important than human life; status-symbols have been more important than brotherhood. To say that in the future we will have to begin giving people priority over things and economic forces is simply to say that a viable future society will have to be humanistically rather than technologically oriented. As Boeing Aircraft discoverd, the fact that we *can* build an SST does not mean that we *must* build it. The fact that we *can* pave over living neighborhoods to make parking lots for suburban commuters does not mean that the advance of the bulldozers is divinely ordained.

Two qualifications. First, it is clear that any future society will be more, not less dependent on technology than the present one. Science is a one-way street. There is no turning back and I hope I have said nothing to suggest that I am advocating a return to the womb. I sympathize with the young people described in Theodore Roszak's *The Making of a Counterculture* and Charles Reich's *The Greening of America*, who think they can solve their problems by homesteading in Alaska or turning on with drugs or joining vegetarian communes. They have their place, and they will doubt-less have some influence on the shape of things to come. But the future that I have in mind presents dangers that can be averted only by the most elegant and precise tools that science, economics, and political philosophy can devise. The question is not whether we need tech-nology but how it is to be used, and this comes back to the problem of things versus people.

Second, when I say that the society of the future will have to be humanistically rather than technologically oriented, I am not calling for a restoration of Plato's philosopher-king or suggesting that English professors should replace politicians in government. What I am say-ing is that those who *do* make decisions, whether they are lawyers or economists or physicists or even English professors, must base their actions on human values rather than economic or technical expedients—on the elemental need to survive, yes; but also on the need to survive with freedom and a sense of human dignity and purpose. This understanding of human values is pre-cisely the aim which humanistic education has always set for itself, whatever its specific accomplishments may or may not have been.

In my opinion I am not simply expressing a pious faith in the humanistic point of view. I have been trying to show that, given the alternatives, a humanistically based culture is the only practical option that we have. This is true whether we are listening to T. S. Eliot or C. P. Snow or the Club of Rome. If we are, indeed, approaching the end of an era, we either set about creating a society based on new values or we passively allow the forces we have created to dominate us in the manner of Mary Shelley's little fable. If our estate has diminished and—to use Ritchie-Calder's phrase—the homestead is mortgaged, we must adjust to the situation or accept foreclosure.

I have spent most of this chapter discussing problems so   IV
large that they can hardly be discussed at all. I make no apology for this. The problems are there. They will not go away, and it is pointless to talk about humanism apart from the context within which humanism functions. Let me now, however, concentrate on matters closer to home.

I assume that there will, in fact, be a future society. I assume that it will be highly technical, but I am willing to believe that it will be a society for human beings rather than the technocratic nightmare described in *1984* or *A Clockwork Orange*. I also assume with the Club of Rome that it will be a society in which opportunities for material satisfaction are limited. The pie will remain about the same size, but the slices will be smaller because more people will demand them.

What are the implications of these assumptions? First, as machines become more efficient and productivity tends to stabilize, the relation between work and leisure will change. This is already happening. We are already paying millions of Americans to stay *out* of the labor market. We call this college education for one group of citizens and welfare for another. College education appears to have a secure future. It will probably expand. But within a few years the concept of welfare with its connotations of the nineteenth-century work ethic will be replaced by the concept of a guaranteed annual income. Welfare aside, the long-term trend for those who have jobs is already toward less work. Vacation periods are being extended, retirement is coming earlier, and, as *Time* Magazine pointed out in a March 1971 feature article entitled "On the Way to the Four Day Week," the work-week is moving toward a norm of four days and thirty-two (or even twenty-eight) hours. These trends are a direct result of the displacement of men by machines. They will continue, perhaps accelerate, as automation becomes more sophisticated. Note that even if you have doubts about the desirability of a society in which useful work is the exception rather than the rule, economic factors seem to be pushing us inexorably in this direction.*

Second, as large numbers of people become less directly and continuously involved in the productive process and as production itself tends to stabilize, the habit of equating success with the accumulation of things will fade. Emphasis will necessarily shift to communal activity in the form of service and to personal, nonutilitarian

*Cf. Max Kaplan and Phillip Bosserman, eds., *Technology, Human Values, and Leisure* (New York: Abingdon, 1972) for further discussion of leisure in the postindustrial era.

forms of satisfaction. As the Meadows observe in *The Limits to Growth*: "Population and capital are the only quantities that need be constant. . . . the pursuits that many people would list as the most desirable and satisfactory activities of man—education, art, music, religion, basic scientific research, and social interactions—could flourish."

Third, whatever the mix that finally evolves—and remember that I am assuming we avoid dangers considered by Lord Snow to be the most serious the race has had to confront—the society I am describing should have a much greater humanistic component than contemporary society. This is true in the simple sense that there will be a larger place in it for humane activity—the "education, art, music, and religion" extolled in *The Limits to Growth*. It is also true in the sense suggested by Immanuel Kant's characterization of humanistic activity as having "purposiveness without purpose"—that is, nonutilitarian, inner-directed activity, with no end beyond itself; activity that resembles play, to use another significant metaphor introduced by Kant, rather than purposive, materially productive labor.

Let me make my point more emphatic. I suggest that the society I am describing will not only value the humanistic point of view, it will be radically humanistic even in its uses of technology. I think that many people are already aware of this fact and are responding to it. I am referring to the response of young people to service programs like the Peace Corps and Vista; the popularity of hiking, bicycling, and camping; burgeoning new religious movements like Catholic Pentecostalism; renewed interest in handicrafts like weaving and pottery and leather working; and the emergence of politically significant opposition to industrial pollution and to technical gymnastics like the space program and the SST. In these tendencies we see, I think, the first half-conscious efforts of masses of people to make a transition from industrial to postindustrial values.

Fourth—and most important from my own point of view—if we *are* on the verge of major social changes, we need to take a very hard look at our educational system. I say this at a time when educational institutions throughout the country, from the public schools to the universities, are facing acute financial difficulties. And I say this at a time when the narrowest and most utilitarian form of education—vocational training—is almost the only form that still receives enthusiastic public support. Nevertheless, if my analysis of the period we are entering is even partially valid, what we do in our educational system is going to play a large part in how well we cope.

It is a truism that a society's educational system is its chief institutional means of shaping its future. To neglect our educational system is to surrender the future to those impersonal and threatening forces that I described earlier. Equally important, to use the educational system to brainwash the young or to discipline them into sullen conformity or to train them for situations that will no longer exist when they are middle-aged is to compound our problems and make theirs intolerable.

We have understood the basic nature of humanistic education since the nineteenth century, and we have learned a great deal about the practice of humanistic education from experiment and research—from Pestalozzi, Montessori, Piaget, Dewey, and more recently from A. S. Neill of Summerhill and Americans like John Holt and George Dennison.* We know that the concept of humanistic education touches every aspect of the schools from financing and administration to architecture, teaching methods, and subject matter. Charles Silberman's *Crisis in the Classroom* is a recent and powerful argument for reshaping the public schools along humanistic lines, coupled with a frightening account of the psychological and social damage caused by authoritarian, prescriptive, and narrowly utilitarian methods.

Apart from the immediate tragedy that it describes, the Scranton Report on Kent State makes a similar point. It underscores the confused, rootless, nearly pathological psychology that develops among students lost in the maze of a large state university. Harsh discipline can doubtless restore order, but it can only intensify confusion and loss of purpose. If we wish something more for our children, our students, and our future citi-

---

*Holt is now so discouraged that he has argued in "The Little Red Prison," in the June 1972 issue of *Harper's*, for the abolition of the school system.

zens, a reshaping of higher education as far-reaching as that proposed by Silberman for the lower schools is needed. It is our best way—institutionally perhaps our only way—of insuring that those who will have to confront the future will possess the means and training to make wise decisions.

V   I have sided here with those who believe we are at a turning point in history. It seems appropriate to add to my own remarks the comment of a great poet on an earlier but perhaps equally momentous turning point in history. John Dryden wrote his *Secular Masque* to welcome New Year's Day of the year 1700. Its most famous passage is spoken by Momus, the god of satire, as a valediction to the age being left behind:

Momus: All, all, of a piece throughout;
[*To Diana*] Thy Chase had a Beast in view;
[*To Mars*] Thy Wars brought nothing about;
[*To Venus*] Thy Lovers were all untrue.
Janus: Tis well an Old Age is out,
All: And time to begin a New.

CHAPTER 6

We shall deserve this reproach as long as we cannot enjoy the beauty of living nature without correcting it, or admire the beauty of imitative art without enquiring after its purpose—as long as we still refuse Imagination any absolute legislative rights of her own.

Schiller, *Letters on the Aesthetic Education of Man*

I suggest that the successors to the present Multiversities will be a congeries of much smaller units marked by a high degree of voluntarism in their membership and a higher degree of agreement on what they are about. . . . These will be the building blocks of any larger educational enterprise.

Martin Trow, speech to the American Council on Education, October, 1970

Only the aesthetic mode of communication unites society, because it relates to that which is common to all.

Schiller, *Letters on the Aesthetic Education of Man*

DEMANDING THE IMPOSSIBLE

A few years ago I began to have doubts about the way I was teaching. It seemed to me that my classes were less exciting than before. The students were polite but slightly withdrawn. Some showed a tendency to lean heavily on the lectures at the expense of the literature being read, a compliment not altogether flattering if the main purpose of a class is to provide stimulus for what goes on outside of class.

The problem was partly my own. There was a general mood of gloom in the air of the academy at the time. Add to a gloomy *Zeitgeist* the fact that I had taught most of my courses for several years. Any time you say the same thing more than two or three times it begins to sound like a cliché.

But a class is never the work of one person. It is a group creation—a *tertium quid* like a play where the end result is the product of text, actors, and audience. The makeup of my audience was changing. When I began teaching, most of my students had been trained in the tradition of formal lectures. They began listening to lectures in high school, and they were taught that if they were inattentive or did not take copious notes they would speedily fail out of college. Lecturing is still common in the secondary schools, but during the sixties many schools began experimenting with less formal kinds of instruction. This was especially true of private schools and the college-preparatory tracks in the suburban public schools. By 1968 many of my students were simply not prepared to sit quietly during fifty minutes of nonstop talk. They might manage physical stasis, but their minds wandered.

I do not mean that all my lectures were nonstop performances. I had tried the question/discussion format with innumerable variations, but there were drawbacks. Take questions. A question can be important or trivial, off the point or on it. The problem is that the lecturer makes judgments about the questions being asked and his judgments are usually—perhaps necessarily—based on his own view of the subject. But the questions come from students, and students are seeking counsel from their point of view, not the lecturer's. For this reason the chances of real communication in the question/discussion format are low. There is a low probability that the lecturer's answer will be meaningful to the student asking the question.

But what, you will ask, about the famous "Socratic" method? My reply is that if you read Plato's *Dialogues*, you quickly discover that the original Socrates was a monster of vanity. He is by turns witty, endearing, wise, and outrageous. He is the star of the show, the arbiter of truth with a capital T and behind his facade of humility he knows it. In real life, trying to maintain the Socratic posture leads teachers to coercion and intellectual hypocrisy. Nobody knows all the answers. If you pretend you do, you make a fool of yourself. The so-called discussion degenerates into a series of mini-lectures, or it rambles on in the faith that if you only keep moving sooner or later you will arrive at a destination. You usually move in circles. As the students realize what is happening they become bored and withdraw mentally, if not in fact. At the end of a typical discussion course they may lack even the semi-coherent notes they could have obtained from a series of formal lectures.

These are only the most obvious of the discontents that finally drove me to reexamine what was happening in the university classroom. I could list many more. Underlying them all is a false but exquisitely seductive assumption. According to this assumption a teacher is a star. The student is by definition an inferior being. His real task—no matter how the cake is frosted—is to learn deference. He may ask polite questions, hat in hand. He may even discuss. But he is always being manipulated, being prodded or led to some preordained conclusion. At the same time, he is required to join in the pretense that he and his peers are free agents.

The result is a system based on falsehood, a con game. Like antigravity, it is antipedagogy. In place of free human communication, you get a master-slave relation that tends to corrupt both sides. Corrupted masters become tyrants—often slothful tyrants—while corrupted slaves become apathetic or rebellious.

I wanted something better. I was scheduled to offer a course in Edmund Spenser just after I began to realize this, so I decided to experiment.

I was fairly certain from previous experience what would happen if I went through the old motions. The students who had registered were a decent lot. I knew that I could count on them to be conscientious. But I knew with equal certainty that given the length of the *Faerie Queene* (some 40,000 lines), their resolution would falter as their responsibilities in other courses— term papers, quizzes, and the like—mounted around mid-semester. Everyone would read books I and II of the *Faerie Queene* (which most of them had already read anyway). But after that the temptation would be to say, "I'll take careful notes. They will make sense of the poem. Then, when I have time, I'll catch up." Nobody ever catches up. At the end of the semester a sizeable percentage of the class would have listened to every lecture but would have read only half of Edmund Spenser.

My basic objective was to beguile my students into reading all of Edmund Spenser. I was quite certain that if they did, they would end with a genuine admiration for his artistry.

On the first day of class I announced that I would provide some introductory lectures (six I think it was). After that I would stop. Instead of relying on me, the class would be taught by a series of two-man teams. Student A would offer a presentation of some aspect of the assigned reading that he considered important. It could be imagery or plot or the relation of the reading assignment to the whole poem or its relation to the history of ideas or its allegorical meaning or its grammar or whatever. There would be only two rules. The subject should be of genuine interest to the speaker, on the assumption that if it bored him it could not help boring us. And the presentation could not last more than twenty minutes, an arrangement that allowed thirty minutes for discussion.

At the end of the presentation, student B would take over. He could comment if he wished for no more than five minutes on the presentation. Then he had to open the floor for discussion and preside, wherever the discussion might lead, until the end of the class period. Meanwhile, I would move to a seat by the window and smoke my pipe. As I look back, I realize that I was proposing to act as referee, or, perhaps more accurately, as the net in an intellectual tennis game. I see this in retrospect. At the time I saw through a glass darkly.

Everybody readily agreed. Nobody, I think, really believed me.

Then the team presentations began. I can confess now that they were wretched. The first speaker summarized a scholarly article written around 1930, with airy asides like "As you all know. . . ." and "As you are aware from having just read scholar Z." This, of course, was blatant hypocrisy. Nobody had read (let alone "just" read) scholar Z. But this was the speaker's idea of a lecture, the distillation, I am sorry to say, of his whole educational experience. The discussion leader then offered an equally grotesque parody of the Socratic discussion method. I puffed my pipe. At the end of the session, I arose, clapped students A and B on the back, and expressed gratification over their fine performances.

For the next two weeks the class dwindled. Students began dropping it. Other muttered darkly about paying good tuition money to take courses from fellow graduate students. The presentations remained tangential, awkward, and topheavy with regurgitated scholarship, while the discussions meandered aimlessly. There were redeeming moments—remember, these were excellent students—but by and large, that is how it was. By the end of the second week of presentations a class of twenty-four had shriveled (as I recall) to twelve. I began to wonder how long the experiment would last. I considered shifting from pipe to cigarettes.

Then, curiously enough, things began to change. The turning point came with a beginning graduate student. This poor innocent had heard so few lectures that he was unable to parody the style. In his naïveté, he simply talked about what he had read, doubtless anticipating withering scorn of his peers. He did not drop a single scholarly name or attempt bibliographical one-upmanship. He did not even imply that he (or his audience) had memorized the reading assignment. It must have been quite a shock when he noticed that everyone was listening.

The discussion that followed the presentation was a great leap forward. Because the presentation had been directly related to the experience of the students as they read the assignment the night before, everyone had a contribution and demanded time to make it.

This is not to write off the earlier sessions as a waste of time. They were not a waste of time. If they did nothing else, they convinced everybody that I was serious—that I was not going to answer questions or manipulate the class in some mysterious nonverbal way. Gradually the class realized that it was on its own. If it failed, the students would have only themselves to blame, which is another way of saying that they were being treated with respect, as adults capable of adult performance and adult responsibility. But the earlier presentations *did* do something more than demonstrate my seriousness. Two weeks of discussion considerably reduced the self-consciousness of the students, their reluctance to say what was really on their minds. In addition, as they became more familiar with each other they began to be aware of each other's interests and special resources. As this happened, people began to speak *to* rather than *at* one another. The group became a social unit, quite different from the classes with which I had previously been familiar; and the discussions became progressively more cooperative and more focused. This is a practical illustration, in little, of the social function of the humanities, and I will return to it later.

Things now improved rapidly. There were ups and downs, but within four more meetings the presentations were uniformly relevant and the discussions lively and pointed. In fact, the discussions grew so lively that they began to spill over the class hour. By mid-semester, debates that started in class tended to continue after class for a half hour or more in the corridor, to the considerable irritation of colleagues whose classes followed mine. Another thing happened. My drop-outs began coming to my office and requesting to be readmitted. Several entirely new faces appeared as auditors. Attendance, which had dwindled to a low of twelve, climbed eventually to thirty, my upper limit in terms of the approach being taken.

Most important, everyone began having fun. Having fun *through* involvement in Spenser rather than in spite of him. I stress this because we sometimes hear that nothing is relevant to students unless it was invented in the twentieth century or can somehow be twisted and reshaped to have twentieth-century application. This was emphatically not true of the Spenser class. Moreover, as the class gained momentum I found myself having as much fun as the students—partly because they were so obviously enjoying themselves, and partly because I began having new thoughts about Spenser myself. You learn something from any class you teach. The Spenser course was especially stimulating because I learned a great deal at almost every meeting. For a change I was listening to other people's ideas instead of repeating things I already knew. At times, I blush to confess, I became so excited that I joined the discussion. But this was well after the class had developed sufficient poise to regard me as an equal rather than an oracle.

Another interesting fact. The first successful presentations were almost pure critical analysis. This was fine as far as I was concerned, since I have always inclined to the belief of the New Critics that the essential act of literary response, and hence of literary criticism, is the confrontation of a text by a sensitive and engaged mind. Literary judgments are essentially subjective. They are not wholly subjective and some are purely and simply wrong, but any response, right or wrong, must take place in the reader's consciousness before it can be defined, communicated, and evaluated. When the quest for objectivity leads to burying a text under mountains of historical, biographical, or philological scholarship, the cart gets put before the horse. The text disappears and the student wanders lost in a maze of secondary literature, much of it dismal in style and dubious in its conclusions. On the other hand, I am not opposed to intelligent use of scholarship. Scholarship is a tool. To reject it out of hand is as arbitrary as it would be for an auto mechanic to foreswear the use of pliers or a doctor the use of adhesive tape. What I noticed in the Spenser class was that as the students became more involved and as they gained confidence, they began to return to scholarship. I think they needed a time to discover where they, themselves, stood in relation to the work they were reading. When they were sure of themselves they could use scholarship without being dominated by it. At any rate, I have the impression that by the last month of the semester they were reading—to use Milton's delightful term—"promiscuously" in the secondary material. And although their judgments of individual books and articles were often quite severe, the mutterings one frequently hears in graduate courses about dry-as-dust pedantry were conspicuous by their absence.

If you are a pragmatist in education you are interested in results. The basic measure of the success of a class is the difference between what students bring to it and what they take away from it. On this basis I consider the Spenser class one of the most successful I have taught. Or the most successful I have not taught. My silence paid off. Term papers and examinations reflected a genuine enthusiasm for the subject, a refreshing independence of the authorities, and most surprisingly, an interest in literary style, the latter being almost unknown in graduate student writing. The story continues beyond term papers and examinations. At the end of the semester about half of the students had become sufficiently addicted to form a "Spenser Circle." They continued to meet during the summer. Late in August they produced a collection of original essays on their poet. Eventually, six of them chose to write dissertations on Spenser. Beyond that and probably much more important, I think that every member of the class left it well equipped to share his enthusiasm with his own future students. The students had gained the knowledge of and respect for Spenser that are the preconditions for successful teaching of an author regardless of the method used. They had also gained experience in teaching through the presentations and discussions. They had a chance—rare enough in graduate education—to try out their own styles of presentation; they also had a chance—nonexistent in most programs—to observe other people's styles and to learn what works and does not work in the interchange between teacher and student.

Why was the experiment successful? I believe it was successful because it came closer to meeting the criteria of humanistic education than most other teaching formats I have tried. I mean humanistic education in the precise philosophical sense, going back to Kant and Schiller, as well as in the looser, more intuitive sense exemplified in A. S. Neill's *Summerhill*, John Holt's *How Children Fail*, and George Dennison's *The Lives of Children.** From the dry, highly technical formulations of the philosophers to the passionate, empirical reports of today's educational reformers, there is general agreement on the basic elements of humanistic education. These are liberation of the imagination, learning as play, and education as communion.

Humanistic education begins by assuming a basic interest or curiosity in every human being. It assumes that

II

*I have been asked whether the method would work for undergraduates or high school students. My answer is that the better the students the less you need to experiment, although I do not believe that merely because a student is good he should be given the worst kind of education we have to offer. The examples of Holt and Dennison, who taught ghetto children, are sufficient to show that the aesthetic approach works with the least promising and most immature students. In fact, it may be the only approach that works with students of this sort.

human beings have a natural and inborn desire to learn and find the right kind of educational experience totally absorbing. They are frustrated, alienated, made hostile by mental blocks created, for example, by psychological conditioning during early childhood or by social fashions like racial prejudice or anti-intellectualism or by authoritarian teaching methods. The foundation on which this analysis rests is the idea of the imagination, which Kant regarded as our most truly human possession. The imagination is born with us. It is the common heritage of all normal human beings. It precedes experience and therefore precedes all psychological conditioning. Experience and conditioning come later. They are obviously necessary. (For example, you have to see one tree before you can think of "tree" as a universal category.) But they always limit the imagination and often in ways that are harmful: "Shades of the prison-house begin to close/Upon the growing Boy." Humanistic education seeks to enlarge the imagination, to remove the bars of the prison house and restore to the individual something like his original birthright. Therefore humanistic education cannot be conceived as a process of filling empty jars with facts, but as a process of removing mental barriers in order to liberate the individual—to help the essentially human element of the mind to attain a greater degree of freedom than it would otherwise have. This concept is the direct opposite of the behaviorist concept of education as "training" or "conditioning."

If the imagination is everyone's birthright, it is possible that except in cases of organic damage "intelligence" as we understand it is a by-product of social factors rather than innate ability. I hesitate to take a position here since I am not an expert. But the point has often been made that the I.Q. tests and College Board examinations on which we once relied so heavily are arbitrary and highly discriminatory.* We know, too, that the most complex thing anybody ever learns is his native language. The whole incredibly complex system that we call language is learned before school begins. It is at least arguable that if an individual can learn to speak English he should find reading or calculus or ancient history easy. If he *does not*, in fact, learn to read or to solve differential equations, it follows that he has been negatively conditioned against learning. The teacher's problem is to remove the negative conditioning. Seen in this light, teaching—as against intimidation—inevitably begins to have a kinship to therapy. This is a conclusion which I resisted for a long time but which I now accept, though with reservations.

To return to the Spenser class, it had obvious affinities to a sensitivity group. My own presence as teacher was felt, but at no time was there an exercise of authority or intimidation. My comments on the presentations

---

*Cf. the criticism by Henry S. Dyer, Vice President of the Educational Testing Service of Princeton, N.J., reported in the education section of the New York *Times* of March 28, 1971, which terms the widely used grade equivalency tests "psychological and statistical monstrosities."

and discussions were limited to encouragement; a way, I suppose, of saying to members of the class, "I am not here to browbeat you or gratify my vanity, but to help you discover your own way into the subject."

The progress of the class, too, followed the pattern of a sensitivity group. Initially there was a period of non-communication. This generated confusion and some hostility (the students who left the class). The problems seemed to increase for several meetings, but there was a counter-current at work. People were gaining confidence and were learning to talk to each other. When the change occurred it was quite sudden. After that, things improved rapidly. People began helping one another instead of practicing one-upmanship. If this analysis is correct, to some degree the mental blocks that stood between the students and the text had been removed. As this happened the natural human delight in something beautiful and profound—Spenser's text—began to emerge.

The removal of limits that circumscribe the imagination can be described as a kind of liberation. This notion goes back to the Kantian idea of the imagination as radically free in the sense of being unconditioned (it precedes personality-formation); and—in relation to the humanities—to the concept of Schiller that art permits a special kind of freedom—*Freiheit in der Erscheinung*—freedom in the world of artistic illusion. Liberation is also a *leitmotif* in the writings of modern educators. Education, they argue, should not serve religion by teaching prescribed moral codes or society by teaching

job skills or scholarship by insisting on specific methodologies or the vanity of the teacher by allowing him to
require conformity to his own version of truth or—as in
the New York State Regents' examinations—versions of
truth that are really transitory educational fashions.
Rather, education should serve individual human beings.
It should help each individual to discover his own resources and interest, recognizing that when he does
this—and probably *only* when he does it—the rest will
follow naturally. Long ago Artistotle spoke of a "natural love of learning" possessed by all men from the slave
to the philosopher. The Kantian equivalent to this idea
is the phrase "purposiveness without purpose." It means
that in aesthetic matters we are moved by our natural
love of the thing itself, not by the use to be made of it
(vocational training) or its "lesson" (education as propaganda) or even by its gratification of the senses (hedon-
ism). In fact, when a program or curriculum is manda-
tory, the natural human response to the subject—the
delight—is often diminished. Learning is then described
as "discipline" or "work" as in "academic discipline"
and "homework." As such ominous words suggest, students have to be driven to this kind of learning by the
system of punishments, overt and covert, that typifies
education today. Most obviously, grades.

In the Spenser class the first step in getting away
from intimidation was removing the teacher from his
symbolic post of authority. The students had to realize
that the success of the class depended on what they, by

free choice, would bring to it; not on a group of lectures that they could transcribe with or without reading the text and then reproduce at examination time. Clearly, it took them a while to get comfortable with this approach. When they did, the result was a remarkable illustration of the possibilities of the liberated imagination. I assume that most of them originally entered the field of English because of a special sensitivity to literature. By the time they reached my class this sensitivity had been so dulled that they distrusted it if they had not forgotten it completely. As they became engrossed in Spenser they rediscovered their original motivations. Discipline became superfluous. The problem for some was that they became so involved in Spenser they had trouble finding time for their other courses.

The liberation extended to methods of approaching Spenser. There was no prescribed method and a great many approaches were used during the semester. Students treated the text in terms of its allegory, in terms of "close reading," in linguistic terms, in relation to the history of ideas, and (in the case of the Amoret and Scudamour episode of *Faerie Queene*, Book III) in terms of ideas about the nature of femininity. Since the class happened to coincide with a widespread campus demand for relevance, I was especially interested to observe that the students, many of whom were converts to the New University Conference, SDS, and Women's Lib, imposed no particular imperative of relevance on themselves. They were liberated, in other words, from their own prescriptions and obsessions as well as mine. It was tacitly assumed that what was most relevant to the class was the developing experience of Spenser's poetry, which is another way of saying that the class naturally tended to purposiveness without purpose, although most of them, I expect, had never heard the term.

A second element that recurs in discussions of humanistic education is the idea of play. Kant first made the comparison of the experience of art to play because play involves the free acceptance of a complex set of rules for the sheer pleasure of the game; and Schiller formalized the metaphor with the term *Spieltrieb*, or "play impulse." Neill and Dennison both remark on the closeness of learning at its best to a game and on the fact that happiness is the hallmark of a good class. Maria Montessori attempted to institutionalize play as a strategy to induce learning. While this seems to me to reverse the cart and the horse—to imply that play is different from learning and to revive the classical metaphor of the bitter pill with the sugar coating—the association of learning with play remains central in the Montessori method today.

I emphasize that the play metaphor applies to adults as well as children. Everyone can recall vivid learning experiences which were also intensely enjoyable. In fact, scientists like Erwin Schrödinger and Werner Heisenberg have written that one of the most powerful motives for scientific research is the pleasure that comes from contemplation of nature's order and variety. Euclid alone,

Edna St. Vincent Millay remarked, has looked on beauty bare.

Certainly, as the Spenser class continued, the students seemed to derive increasing personal pleasure from the experience of the poetry. This, I suppose, is what the play theory is all about whether you are experiencing a work of art or playing a game of chess. The play theory has an important corollary. In great poetry—even in a tragedy like *King Lear*—there is a dazzling virtuosity of language, a playfulness, that is fully consonant with the tragic theme. By the same token, in a successful class the pleasure that comes from an increasing sense of rapport with the subject can spill over into spontaneous wit, intellectual arabesques, and various informal games that develop among those involved. This situation is characteristic of the free play of the mind. Where it does not occur there is at least a suspicion that the free play of the mind is being repressed.

Third, humanistic education, when successful, encourages both communication and communion. Speaking generally, it is here, I think, that we find the true social function of the humanities, especially of those works that a culture designates its classics. If you can discuss Pushkin with a Russian or James Baldwin with a black or Dante with an Italian or *Rashomon* with a Japanese, you share a culture. You have a common bond, a medium within which you can explore your differences and similarities. At the least you communicate. At best a deeper relationship that might be called communion can develop. To return to the classroom which was my laboratory for observing humanistic education in practice, as the semester progressed it was very obvious that the students became more tolerant and understanding of one another. In several cases deeper bonds of affection—something like a genuine communion—developed. I will add that if the most obvious form of communion in humanistic education is lateral, between those who share cultural experiences, another more subtle but equally important form of communion also occurs. I mean the communion of the present with the past—the sense of unity with tradition that comes from experiencing great works of the past.

The concept of humanistic education invariably raises III questions about standards. If you are not prescriptive, if you do not encourage competition through examinations and grading, how can you be sure that you are really educating people?

One answer to this is that current testing methods are at best dubious. Another answer, more to the point, is that if a teacher does not know how he is doing without the chinoiserie of drills, quizzes, tests, and grades, it is questionable whether he belongs in a classroom.

The fact is that most so-called standards are arbitrary. Their real reason for existence is not to insure excellence but to provide a basis for intimidation that can later be used to force people into slots in the social pecking order. The only valid standard in humanistic education is "How much has this student developed his own interests? How much growth has occurred in this course?" The Spenser course convinced me that this standard is not only humane but also efficient, for it produced more effort and more assimilation than all the psychological thumbscrews currently favored by the educational establishment. But you cannot express this standard as a grade-point average or a letter in a grade book.

One caution. The approach I am describing will not work with large classes, nor will it work with teachers so committed to their own private views of a subject that they cannot be comfortable with other human beings except in a master-slave relation. Nor, obviously, will it work with teachers who are ignorant of what they are teaching. If you are talking about something it is always desirable to know what you are talking about.

The tragedy of the current economic woes of the schools is that they make humanistic method more and more difficult. The trend is to large classes, vocational training, cheaper (that is, less well-trained) teachers, cost-accounting, and the alleged efficiencies of canned materials and teaching machines. This is a prime example of what I referred to in the preceding chapter as the habit of technological society of giving precedence to economic rather than human values. My point then was that the priorities have to be reversed in the interest of a possible future society. I will add that an expensive educational system that fails to educate is surely less of a bargain than a more expensive one that works.

This leads me to the shape of higher education in the future. It will be obvious from what I have said that I believe we should have more, not less of the humanistic element in every aspect of higher education. Here I join a vocal band of educators, students, and laymen who have attacked the multiversity and all its works—its computer lockstep, its indifference to human beings, and its tendency to organize all knowledge into departments which eventually become factories to produce graduate students. IV

The basic requirement is to think small. The university needs to develop sub-units adjusted to the human scale of life while remaining permeable in both directions to the outside world. This is not the place to discuss co-op programs and residence and cluster colleges, but the popularity of such experiments reveals the scope of current disenchantment with bigness and bureaucracy. I would also be reluctant to guess what size an ideal educational unit should be. As a rule of thumb it should be small enough to be a community. If it fails to be a community it has failed in the task for which it was created in the first place. I lean to smallness, but I realize that some communities are quite large.

And the curriculum? Clearly it should be flexible. Students should be more important than the pious lies in the catalogue. But there is another side to the coin. Flexibility does not mean formlessness. The curriculum should be a program not a collection of courses, and the program should express a thoughtful, well-articulated educational philosophy. Personally, I feel that students need as comprehensive an understanding as possible of the world they will enter after graduation and I therefore favor broadly defined requirements in the sciences, the social sciences, and the humanities.

Within these limits the humanities can play a unique and vitally important role. The humanities are the least esoteric subjects in the curriculum. Clerk Maxwell's thermodynamic equations are intrinsically beautiful, but to appreciate their beauty you need at least two years of calculus. You do not, however, need to know marble from granite to appreciate Michelangelo's *David*, or how to play the scales to enjoy a Mozart trio. Intensive study of a science—that is, specialization—leads to experiences that can be shared with fewer and fewer people. Specialization is necessary in an advanced culture but inevitably it divides people. The humanities tend to unite people—the idea of community again.

In 1936, when World War II was already visible on the horizon, Benedette Croce wrote an essay *On Poetry* in which he attacked the academy for its betrayal of human values. By fragmenting humanistic studies, he warned, the academy was contributing to the dismemberment of the human spirit by ideology:

Not only is beauty no longer one and indivisible, but its divisions are no longer those of dramatic and lyric, ingenuous and sentimental, classical and romantic, which though arbitrary were in intention universally human. Its divisions are now the people themselves and the social classes with whose doings the work of poetry is identified; hence the category of judgment is by turns

Germany, France, England, Russia, Italy, or bourgeoise, democracy, sickle and hammer, Swastika, and so forth.

Such divisions do not merely, like the older ones, break up the aesthetic unity of the human race, but they destroy humanity itself by confining it to regions that are foreign to one another and irreconcilably and perpetually hostile.

Schiller believed that the problem of politics can be solved only through the problem of the aesthetic. His idea sounds naive if not absurd at first, but the more one ponders it the less absurd it becomes. In a culture corrupted by things and fragmented by abstractions and ideologies the social task of the humanities is to remind us that the life of humanity is the life of the spirit and that beyond all our differences we share a single community—what Croce called the aesthetic unity of the human race and what Schiller defined as the beauty by which man makes his way to freedom. It is possible to state these concepts in the abstract and technical language of philosophy, but they can also be as real and as immediate as a class in a single, little-read English poet.

Am I asking too much of the humanities? Perhaps. But whatever we do in the future it will be because we have chosen to do it, and we will choose, rightly or wrongly, on the basis of our idea of humanity. We cannot escape our freedom any more than we can escape the tragic dignity that comes from living with the consequences of our choices. The inscription over the entrance of Dante's Hell reads:

Abandon hope all ye who enter here.

I prefer the motto scrawled by the students of Paris on the time-blackened walls of the Sorbonne:

Be realistic. Demand the impossible.

INDEX

159

Ulysses, 33

Vergil, 41, 68
Verlaine, Paul, 20
Verrocchio, Andrea del, 63
Vogelweide, Walther von der, 44

Wald, George, 113
Ward, Barbara, 113
Warren, Robert Penn, 52

Wilder, Billy, 56
Williams, Aubrey, 19
Wilson, Thomas, 66, 67, 77
Winckelmann, Johann Joachim, xvii
Woodrow Wilson Foundation, 13
Wordsworth, William, 46, 96

Yeats, William Butler, 54
York, Harold, 113, 114

THE JOHNS HOPKINS UNIVERSITY PRESS

This book was composed in Aldine Roman text and Baskerville display
by Jones Composition Company from a design by Laurie Jewell.
It was printed by The Murray Printing Company on 60-lb. Perkins and
Squier Special Book paper in a natural shade. The cloth edition was
bound by Moore and Company in Joanna Kennett cloth and Kivar Victoria.
The paperback edition was bound by The Murray Printing Company.

Library of Congress Cataloging in Publication Data

Hardison, O   B
 Toward freedom and dignity.

 "Originally delivered as a group of lectures at the annual Humanities
Forum sponsored by Elon College in North Carolina."
 1. Education, Humanistic. I. Title.
LC1011.H263 370.11'2 72-4010
ISBN 0-8018-1415-4
ISBN 0-8018-1416-2 (pbk)

DATE DUE

GAYLORD   PRINTED IN U.S.A.